Essential Table Service

Essential Table Service
for restaurants

A new version of the standard textbook *The Waiter*

John Fuller

Hutchinson

London   Melbourne   Sydney   Auckland   Johannesburg

Hutchinson Education
An imprint of Century Hutchinson Limited
62–65 Chandos Place, London WC2N 4NW

Century Hutchinson Group (Australia) Pty Ltd
16–22 Church Street, Hawthorn, Melbourne, Victoria 3122

Century Hutchinson Group (NZ) Ltd
32–34 View Road, PO Box 40–086, Glenfield, Auckland 10

Century Hutchinson (SA) (Pty) Ltd
PO Box 337, Bergvlei 2012, South Africa

First published 1986

Designed by Roger Walker

Typeset in 10/12 pt English Times Compugraphic by
Colset Private Limited, Singapore
Printed and bound in Great Britain by Anchor Brendon Ltd, Tiptree, Essex

British Library Cataloguing in Publication Data
Fuller, John, *1916*–
Essential table service: for restaurants.
——Updated ed.
1. Table service
I. Title   II. Fuller, John, *1916*–
Waiter
642′.6   TX925
ISBN 0-09-164791-6

Contents

Preface

A plan to develop *The Waiter* resulted in the enlarged *Modern Restaurant Service*, published by Hutchinson in 1983. The reception accorded this more advanced text indicated that it met a need. Yet continuing demand for *The Waiter*, an accepted text since 1947, suggested an additional need to update this primer *as* a primer.

First overhauled in 1965, twenty years later the book has again undergone extensive revision. Hence, substantially adapted and with additional material, this new version is re-titled *Essential Table Service*.

The title change emphasizes the book's role (like that of the original edition) as a basic text to guide hotel and catering students, waiters and waitresses in the essential elements of waiting practice. It also aims to provide details of restaurant service procedures to others entering the catering industry or on basic catering courses.

This basic primer, *Essential Table Service*, deals with fundamental waiting. *Modern Restaurant Service* covers further details of restaurant practice. Any small overlap between the two does not, I believe, invalidate the objective that the books should complement each other.

I trust that the part *The Waiter* has fulfilled for forty years in restaurant service training may continue in its new form as *Essential Table Service*.

John Fuller
Oxford, 1986.

Acknowledgements

This primer began life as a textbook sponsored by the then Hotel and Catering Institute and several distinguished members, led by the late O.G. Goring and the late N.L.W. Barratt, contributed to former versions. I am grateful for help accorded in the previous version of *The Waiter* by Mr. A.J. Currie, formerly lecturer in catering at the Scottish Hotel School, Strathclyde University. I thank the following companies, organizations and persons for permission to reproduce illustrations and for providing menus.

M. Anton Mosimann, Maître Chef de Cuisine, The Dorchester, London W1.
The Press Office, The Savoy, The Strand, London WC2
The Press Office, The Ritz Hotel, Piccadilly, London W1
The Press Office, The Strand Palace Hotel, London WC2
NCR Limited, 206 Marylebone Road, London NW1 6LY
Cona Coffee Machine Company, Felden Works, Railway Place, Wimbledon SW19 3RS
The Health Education Council, Bloomsbury, London WC1X 0HD

Every effort has been made to reach copyright holders but the publishers would be grateful to hear from any source whose copyright they may have unwittingly infringed.

Finally, I again acknowledge the invaluable cooperation of my wife at all stages of the production of this book.

1
Restaurants: Waiters' Workplaces

There are many kinds of catering establishment. In some, food is collected by diners themselves from a servery. This self-service or cafeteria style is widespread in industrial and institutional operations and is also featured in some commercial restaurants and cafés. However, in a vast number of restaurants, coffee shops and other kinds of meal outlets, food is served by waiters or waitresses.

This book is concerned with those who undertake this important food and beverage service. (Food and beverage staff include just as many women as men and throughout the book where the word waiter is used, it refers also to waitresses, unless otherwise stated.)

Restaurant — a sales area

The 'front of the house' (in this case the restaurant, coffee shop or dining room) is a marketing or sales area. Behind the scenes (e.g. the kitchen, stillroom, dispense bar or cellars), simple or complicated activity produces what is to be sold, that is, served to customers. The waiter's prime task, therefore, is to sell the restaurant product. This product comprises not only food and beverages, but the service itself, that is, the way a customer's experience in the restaurant is 'packaged'. Decor, styling and amenities all play their part in this 'package' (Figure 1). Customers buy not only food and drink, but a complete dining 'experience'.

When, as a member of a restaurant's service staff, you understand your 'product' and the significance of your work in a sales team, you will find it easier to appreciate details which require your attention. Think of what you expect from anyone whose job is to sell you goods or service. Apart from his having knowledge of the product to be sold, one would expect the salesman to be pleasant, of good appearance, well-mannered and enthusiastic about what he has to sell. Thus, in waiting, in addition to skills of serving, one needs to cultivate personal qualities to become an effective restaurant salesman.

Management's contribution to marketing is not deeply explored here; however, in deciding on what kind of restaurant to run and how to run it,

Figure 1   The Ritz restaurant exemplifies ambience based on traditional elegance.

management must give thought to the wants of their desired customers in order to evolve policies and procedures based on careful planning. In turn, their staff should seek to understand the nature of the business, the kind of customer catered for and how best to meet the customer's requirements; for as salesmen waiters assist materially in merchandising.

Ambience

A successful catering operation is one to which guests want to return and where they feel at ease. Food and beverage success depends on three components: management, production staff (cooks) and sales staff (waiters). Each plays a different role, but they are all part of one team. All staff must possess the following attributes: interest in their work; pride in the firm; and loyalty to the firm.

A restaurant's atmosphere or personality depends on:

- welcoming staff and their skills and product knowledge
- good food and tactful advice in selecting from the menu
- friendly, courteous, quiet, efficient but unostentatious service
- pleasant surroundings

This latter, whether a simple coffee shop or an up-market gourmet restaurant, is achieved through:

- design (with the aid of an architect and other specialists)
- décor (wall covering, curtains, paints, etc.)
- furniture, equipment and appointments
- lighting

By these amenities both buyer and seller are satisfied and the goodwill of the business increased.

The waiter's role

At a time when many jobs are becoming increasingly monotonous, catering offers variety. Waiters and waitresses are in contact with a wide range of people, all with different interests; this helps them to develop tact and initiative, keep their minds active and to express their personalities.

A waiter in his contact with guests represents the owners. He contributes to the image of the establishment and much of its success depends on his skills, interest and qualities.

Advancement

Waiting holds promising career possibilities. Many proprietors started as junior waiters. Every restaurant manager's knowledge and skill is based on experience in waiting for there is no short cut to management. One cannot just 'drop into' management, but it is worth starting a climb because a restaurateur can command a high salary and a respected status.

Nearly all posts of head waiter (or head waitress), maître d'hôtel, or restaurant manager are obtained by those who have learned by training and experience the best ways to do the work which they organize. This also applies to many owners of catering establishments. Good service is sought everywhere so that a good waiter always has opportunities for promotion.

Types of establishment

Once the aims of an operation are grasped, the importance of personal appearance and style within the appropriate atmosphere of formality or informality are more easily assessed.

There are wide variations in types of restaurant (Figure 2). Some are virtually in show business; their customers want to see and be seen. A restaurant where dishes are perhaps flamed at the table and where the meal-time occupies the best part of the evening, provides as much entertainment as nourishment. By contrast, a business lunch may require a different kind of efficiency to achieve speedy customer turnover.

Listing all possible types of establishment is not necessarily helpful. Large and expensive hotels may operate restaurants to meet gourmet requirements, but also may run middle- or even low-cost, fast food operations like coffee shops. In the right location, a pub may develop a restaurant to benefit from waiting skills.

Waiters as merchandizers

Whatever the level of service, meals need to be merchandized. Principles applied in making products attractive in retail outlets like supermarkets, multiple stores and other shops also apply in merchandizing a meal. Cus-

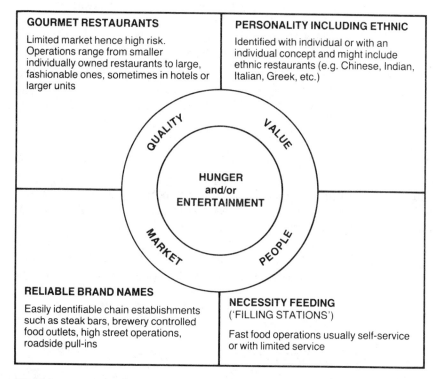

All catering operations aim to meet the customer's need to satisfy his hunger and/or his wish to be 'entertained'. Caterers must, therefore, identify the people who will make up their market and then meet that market by quality and value for money.

The division of catering market into four quarters in *Figure 1*, is merely one way of indicating how the catering market is varied. Trends change but the numbers of those eating out or away from home continue to grow.

Figure 2   Who and where do waiters serve?

tomers may buy on impulse in retail outlets because the product looks good, that is, it is well presented or packaged. Similar concepts are valid in restaurants — from up-market (fashionable or gourmet) places to simpler coffee shops with a brisk trade. What looks good and can readily be seen to be good depends, in those operations which employ waiting staff, on presentation through their salesmanship skills.

Operations continue to change. Steak bars may be popular for a period, but then may need to be modified. Carveries fulfill many criteria for visual appeal, but how they are operated may be varied after a time. Detailed listing of all the kinds of operation in which waiters do their job is less important than recognition of the variables from up-market to modest establishments. Figure 1 gives some indication of how customer requirements may be identified and met.

All catering operations aim to meet the customer's need to satisfy his hunger and/or his wish to be 'entertained'. Caterers must, therefore, identify the people who will make up their market and then meet that market by quality and value for money.

The division of the catering market into four quarters in Figure 1 is merely one way of indicating how the catering market is varied. Trends change but the number of those eating out or away from home continues to grow.

2
Product Knowledge I: Kitchen Basics

The waiter deals with a complex product. Food and beverages loom large in it, but a waiter also sells intangible elements within the service he provides. Later chapters deal with tasks involving welcome, courtesy and other elements less tangible than food and drink. Nevertheless, competent waiting staff should acquire sound knowledge of the product sold.

It is helpful to understand how professional kitchens developed and dishes were created. Kitchen brigades were originally devised to effect à la carte service from a menu of many choices in the French style. In services of set menus (table d'hôte) of modest scope, the same amount of specialization is not required and cooks can combine duties to reduce the number of sections. Modern menus of more limited choice do not require all the staff of a large, traditional, French-style kitchen. In the latter, there may be the following staff.

The chef (or head chef) – chef de cuisine (or maître chef). In control of all the sections and their chefs (parties and chefs de parties).

Sauce cook – chef saucier. Makes sauces for savoury dishes and prepares entrées; possibly acts as sous chef (principal assistant to the chef de cuisine).

Larder cook – chef garde manger. In charge of the 'cold kitchen', preparation of hors d'oeuvre, cold meats, canapés, sandwiches, salads, mayonnaise, dressings, etc.; preparation of cuts of meat, fish, poultry and game for other parties; may act as sous chef.

Vegetable cook – chef entremettier. Cooks vegetables, egg dishes and farinaceous dishes (Italian pastas, etc.) including vegetable garnishes.

Soup cook – chef postager. Prepares soups.

Roast cook – chef rôtisseur. Roasts meat and poultry and prepares savouries, grilled dishes (there might also be a subordinate grill cook – chef grillardin) and deep fried potatoes.

Fish cook – chef poissonier. Prepares fish dishes and their accompanying sauces.

Pastry cook – chef pâtissier. In charge of the pâtisserie; preparation of sweet dishes and desserts including pastry, cakes, jellies and ices.

Relief cook — chef tournant. Relieves other chefs de partie on their days off, sickness, holiday, etc.

Staff cook — chef communar. In charge of staff catering.

Breakfast cook. Early duty cook (often of limited training) who prepares breakfast dishes.

Storekeeper — l'économe. In charge of commodity store.

Support staff. In a large operation like a high class hotel restaurant chefs may have one or more commis (assistants). The brigade of chefs is supported by kitchen porters, vegetable preparation assistants, pot washers (plongeur) and kitchen clerks. Of the latter, the following comes into contact with waiting staff.

Announcer — Aboyeur (literally 'barker'). The kitchen clerk who calls out to the kitchen orders brought by waiters to the servery.

Stillroom staff. Responsible for hot beverages, toasts, etc. Stillroom staff are not traditionally regarded as part of the kitchen brigade but, like the silver and plate wash, are usually supervised by the restaurant manager or maître d'hôtel. Stillroom work is discussed further in Chapters 16 and 17.

Names in food and cookery

The chefs brigade structure indicates the possible complexity of the cuisine. A chef needs years of training and experience. The waiter need not know about cookery in the same way; he should, however, understand elements that affect his work, for instance:

- how much time will elapse between ordering a dish and its being served
- when foods are in season
- basic modes of cooking
- the meaning of common terms, usually French, on the menu

The most useful words are those for common foods (e.g. the meats, cuts, vegetables, etc.), styles of cooking (boiled, grilled, etc.) and modes of dressing or garnishing.

Modes of cooking

Some basic information about foods, cooking times and terms is given in Tables 1—4 on pp. 8—11 but modes of dressing dishes as codified in repertoires of 'classic' cookery number many hundreds.

Professional cookery of the western world evolved in France; so that the culinary code is fundamentally French. Some preparations may be peasant (à la paysanne) style, others bourgeois (à la bourgeoise) or linked with hunting (chasseur).

Dish styles may be named for people (Henry IV, Rossini, Melba, etc.), others for kinds of people (e.g. *à la reine* (queen), *à la princesse* (princess)), for places (perhaps where the food flourished, e.g. Argenteuil for asparagus), for battles (Marengo and Creçy), or after chefs or their places of work (e.g. Reform (from the Reform Club) or Carême (after the great Regency chef)).

Spelling variations

Styles of cooking usually appear on menus as a past participle describing a noun; for example rôti meaning roasted) is the past participle of rôtir, to roast. It describes gigot (meaning leg) in the phrase: gigot d'agneau rôti. Gigot is a masculine, singular noun but when rôti has to describe a feminine noun it will change by the addition of 'e' for feminine and 's' for plural, or both 'es' for feminine plural — hence pommes rôties for roasted potatoes.

There will be such changes in spelling on menus; but participles in Tables 1 and 2 are in the simple masculine singular.

Table 1   Basic modes of cooking.

Braiser	To braise, by oven cooking in enclosed pot. Hence braisé — braised
Bouillir	To boil by immersion in boiling water, stock or other liquid. Hence bouilli — boiled
Étuver	To stew by gentle simmering (often in food's own juice or a little added liquor). Hence étuvé — stewed
Frire	To deep fry by immersion in hot fat or oil. Hence frit — fried
Griller	To grill or broil, similar to true roasting but for smaller cuts, i.e. cooking on gridiron over clear fire (often charcoal, gas or electric radiants). Hence grillé — grilled or broiled
Pocher	To poach by gentle cooking in boiling liquid. Hence poché — poached
Poêler	To pot roast in covered pan on bed of roots. Hence poêlé — pot roasted
Rôtir	To roast, cooking by radiant heat before or over a clear fire. (Nowadays, food is often 'roasted' in the dry heat of an oven). Hence rôti — roasted
Sauter	To shallow fry (literally to jump or toss) in pan with a smaller quantity of fat or oil. Hence sauté — shallow fried
En vapeur	To cook in steam. Hence vapeur or en vapeur — steamed

Further modes of cooking

Derivative from the basic styles listed in Table 1 are other modes of cooking expressed by French terms. Table 2 lists a selection of these terms.

Table 2 French terminology used in cooking.

Ail, à l'	With garlic
Anglaise, à l'	In English style, i.e. plainly roasted, boiled, fried with simple English accompaniments
Aspic, en	Cold in aspic or jelly
Broche, à la	On the spit, i.e. roasted
Brochette, à la	On a skewer, i.e. grilled or broiled
Casserole, en	Braised or stewed within an enclosed fireproof dish
Coquille, en	Cooked in shell (usually in a scallop shell)
Croquette	Minced, shaped as large corks and fried
Croustade, en	In pastry
Diablé	Devilled, highly seasoned
Emincé	Minced
Farci	Stuffed
Froid	Cold
Fines-herbes	With finely chopped herbs
Flambé	Flamed
Frappé	Chilled
Fumé	Smoked
Garni	Garnished
Gelée, en	In jelly
Glacé	Glazed or iced
Gratin, au	Breadcrumb-topped and glazed
Hachi	Minced
Jus, au	With its natural juice or liquor
Maigre, au	Without meat, Lenten fare
Meunière	Shallow fried (fish) in butter, lemon garnish
Naturel, au	In simple or natural style
Orly, à l'	Fried in batter (tomato sauce separately)
Purée, en	Mashed or puréed
Refraîchi	Lightly chilled
Réchauffé	Reheated
Tasse, en	In cup
Terrine, en	In earthenware dish (usually a pâté)
Vert-pré	With watercress (usually grills)

Degrees of cooking

The terms listed in Table 3 apply especially to grilling.

Table 3   Terminology used for grilled food.

à point	Medium grilled, just done
Bleu	Very underdone, i.e. charred outside and raw or 'blue' inside
Bien cuit	Well cooked
Flared	As bleu
Rare	Underdone
Saignant	Underdone

Cooking times for à la carte service

A customer ordering à la carte often states his requirements in advance of the meal to give adequate time for the kitchen to prepare the dishes.

Microwave, infra-red or radar range equipment usage alters cooking times; however, Table 4 lists the approximate times between a waiter giving an à la carte order to the kitchen and its being ready for service.

Table 4   Cooking times between à la carte order and service.

Dish	Time (Minutes)
Clear soup (consommé)	10
Thick soup (crème)	10
Macaroni, spaghetti (in butter or tomato sauce)	15
Omelette, fried eggs	10
Bacon and eggs (oeufs au lard)	10
Poached or scrambled eggs (oeufs pochés ou brouillés)	10
Fish, fried or grilled	10–15
Fish, poached	20
Calf's liver (foie de veau)	15
Châteaubriand	20
Grills:	
Steaks	
Underdone (rare)	10
Medium	15
Well done	20
Lamb chop (chop d'agneau)	15
Mutton chop (chop de mouton)	15–20
Pork cutlet (côtelette de porc)	20
Veal cutlet (côtelette de veau)	20

Game	25–40
Pigeon, roasted or grilled	25
Roast game birds (for small birds)	from 12
Roast game birds (for larger varieties)	up to 45
Spring chicken (1 portion (poussin) or two portions (poulet de grain)	20–30
Chicken (3 to 4 portions (poulet)	45–60
Chicken en cocotte (poulet en cocotte)	40
Chicken wing fillet (suprême de volaille)	20
Potatoes, fried (pommes frites)	20
Potatoes, mashed (pommes en purée)	10
Potatoes, sautées (pommes sautées)	10
Potatoes, boiled (pommes nature)	10
Tomatoes, grilled (tomates grillées)	10
Soufflé	35

Foods in season

'In season' used to imply that foods were served only at that time of the year, for example, in Britain grouse is first shot on 12 August and the oyster season opens on 1 September. Freezing and cold storage has lengthened or eliminated seasons for many foods. Tables 5–9 give details of all the different foods and their seasons.

Table 5 Fish in season.

Oyster (huitres)	September – April
Mussels (moules)	September – April
Mackerel (maquereau)	April – October
Salmon, Scotch (saumon d'Écosse)	February – August
Salmon (English)	March – September
Salmon trout (truite saumonée)	March – September
River trout (truite)	April – September
Sole (sole); Cod (cabillaud); Whiting (merlan); Haddock (aigrefin (*alt.* aiglefin); Herrings (harengs); Turbot (turbot); Halibut (flétan), etc.	All the year

Table 6 Poultry in season.

Spring chicken, poussin	April – June
Duck, chicken, capon, (canard, poulet, chapon)	All the year
Turkey (dinde)	All the year
Gosling (oison)	April – September
Goose (oie)	December

Table 7 Game in season.

Snipe, Woodcock (bécassine, bécasse)	October – March
Quail (farmed or imported) (caille)	All the year
Wild duck (caneton sauvage)	In autumn and winter
Venison (venaison)	July – February
Pheasant (faisan)	1 October – February
Grouse (coq de bruyère)	12 August – December
Hares (lièvres)	August – February
Partridges (perdreaux)	1 September – February
Plovers (pluviers)	October – March

Table 8 Vegetables (fresh) in season.

Artichokes (artichauts)	November – June
Jerusalem artichokes (topinambours)	Autumn – winter
Asparagus, natural (asperges)	May – August
Celery (céleri)	September – March
Seakale (chou de mer)	December – May
Sprouts (choux de Bruxelles)	September – March
Marrow (courgette)	July – October
Broad beans (féves)	June – August
French beans (haricots verts)	June – September
New peas (petits pois)	May – July
Truffle, fresh (truffe)	Autumn – winter
Chicory (endive)	October – March

Table 9 Fruits in season.

Cherries (cerises)	May – July
Green figs (figues vertes)	In autumn
Strawberries, forced and natural (fraises)	In summer
Raspberries (framboises)	In summer
Gooseberries and currants (groseilles à maquereau and groseilles)	In summer
Tangerines (mandarines)	November – June
Melon (melon)	All the year
Plums (prunes)	July – October
Rhubard, forced and natural (rhubarbe)	January – June

3
Product Knowledge II: Menus

The work of the kitchen finds ultimate expression in the menu which indicates to customers the nature of the establishment and what is available.

Composition of a meal

When its various courses are carefully balanced, a meal pleases a diner without his feeling overfed. Otherwise, even if excellent individually, a series of dishes may make an unattractive and indigestible meal.

Banquet

A banquet is the longest meal served. The order of dishes may include some or all of the following.

- A small dish to stimulate appetite (hors d'oeuvre, soup, etc.)
- A light food course (such as fish with appropriate sauce)
- Followed by a light meat course (the entrée)
- Sometimes service of a sorbet may provide a pause for re-stimulation of appetite
- The main dish (roast served with a salad or possibly with vegetable and potatoes)
- A light sweet or ice
- A choice of dessert, fruit or cheese
- Coffee

Chapter 18 gives further details of wines which follow the order given below — from stimulation to satisfaction of appetite.

- Light wines (usually white)
- Heavier wines
- Until coffee is served, often accompanied by brandy or a liqueur

Dinner

Dinner (implying an ordinary meal of the day, served usually in the evening) is seldom so elaborate as a banquet and some courses are normally omitted. An example of an à la carte dinner menu is given in Figure 3. (See Figure 6 for a table d'hôte menu.)

Nevertheless, evening dinner is longer and more leisurely (usually having more courses) than luncheon; although modern customers dining informally seldom select more than three, at most four, courses from the following.

- Hors d'oeuvres, especially single ones such as cantaloup melon, smoked salmon (saumon fumé) or prawns (crevettes roses)
- A choice of a thick or clear soup (served *en tasse*, in a cup)
- Poached fish with or in a sauce, or if fried, small fish such as blanchailles (whitebait) or fillets of sole cut in strips (en goujons)
- An entrée
- A roast garnished with pommes soufflés, or pommes chips accompanied with salad
- A sweet, for example an ice cream dish in a coupe and/or a savoury
- Coffee. Brandy and liqueurs passed

For an especially elaborate function dinner an organizer may add:

- a remove or relevé to follow the entrée
- a sorbet before the roast
- an extra fine vegetable course (asparagus or globe artichokes) to follow the roast

Wine is invariably taken, with brandy or liqueurs to follow. Dishes are garnished with accompaniments, presented (to the left of the host) and, as appropriate, carved or portioned in front of the table.

Luncheon

Midday luncheon is shorter and simpler, generally consisting of three or at most four courses.

- Hors d'oeuvres or choice of thick or clear soup
- Fish, egg or rice or a pasta dish
  and/or
- A roast joint, a grill or a prepared meat dish such as a stew, offal dish, chicken pie or a choice from the Cold Buffet
- Sweets
  and/or
- Cheese with celery and biscuits

Figure 4 is an example of an à la carte luncheon menu. (See Figure 5 for a table d'hôte menu.)

Diner

Goutte d'Or aux Quenelles à la Moëlle
(BEEF CONSOMMÉ WITH MARROW DUMPLINGS)

Filets de Sole aux Beurre Blanc et d'Echalotes
Rouges
(FILLETS OF SOLE WITH WHITE BUTTER SAUCE
AND RED WINE SHALLOTS)

Crèpinettes de Côtelette d'Agneau au
Choux Braisé
(STUFFED LAMB CUTLET WITH BRAISED CABBAGE)

Compote de Fruits "Dorchester" C.N.

Café

Délice des Dames

(£24.00 PER PERSON, INCLUSIVE OF SERVICE & V.A.T.)

Pour Commencer

Saumon d'Ecosse Mariné   £9.20
(SCOTTISH SALMON MARINATED WITH
HERBS AND YOGHURT DRESSING)   C.N.

Parfait de Foies de Volaille   £5.50
aux Truffes
(DELICIOUS CHICKEN LIVER TERRINE WITH TRUFFLES)

Aiguillettes de Saumon Glacées £7.50
à l'Oseille
(WILD SCOTCH SALMON GLAZED WITH SORREL SAUCE)

Salade d'Asperges et Coquilles St Jacques £6.70
(ASPARAGUS SALAD WITH SAUTÉED SCALLOPS)

Feuilleté de Ris de Veau aux   £6.00
Ecrevisses
(CALF'S SWEETBREADS WITH CRAYFISH IN
PUFF PASTRY)

Symphonie de Fruits de Mer   £6.70
"Naturelle"   C.N.
(A VARIETY OF SEAFOOD IN ITS OWN JUICE)

Menu Surprise

Six delicious light courses of
fresh produce from the Market

(£58.00 FOR TWO PERSONS
INCLUSIVE OF SERVICE AND V.A.T.)

Potages

Crème de Cresson et Pommes de   £4.60
Terre aux Quenelles de Saumon Fumé
(CREAM SOUP OF WATERCRESS & POTATOES
WITH QUENELLES OF SMOKED SALMON)

Goutte d'Or aux Quenelles à la Moëlle   £4.00
(BEEF CONSOMMÉ WITH MARROW DUMPLINGS)

Potage de Concombre Froid   £3.50
(CHILLED CUCUMBER SOUP)

ALL PRICES ARE INCLUSIVE OF SERVICE & V.A.T.

Figure 3 Example of an à la carte dinner menu, The Terrace Restaurant, The Dorchester.

Figure 3 *Cont'd*

Covers for luncheon and dinner

Table and room lay-out vary according to the type of business. Up-market restaurants may lay tables for hors d'oeuvres only, that is a fish knife and fork, a cover plate with a simply folded napkin, and a side plate with a roll and small knife on it.

On the table will be centred a cruet, with a flower vase behind and ashtray in front of it. One wine glass on the right-hand side above the knife, toast Melba on a plate with a d'oyley, butter (with ice) and butter knife on a service plate placed on the table when the guests are seated.

In popular operations there may be a full lay-up, that is a large knife and fork on the side of the cover plate, fish knife and fork outside these, a soup spoon to the right of the fish knife. On the side plate, a bread roll with a small knife and dessert service in front of the plate. On the table, butter dish, cruets, glass, ashtray, and vase of flowers. Toast Melba may not be offered in such establishments.

The courses

The number of courses served varies with meals (whether lunch, dinner or supper), type of restaurant, numbers catered for and price charged. The sequence, outlined above, in which dishes are served is, however, followed no matter how long or short the menu.

The following summarizes the nature of possible courses but it is again stressed that a full dinner is nowadays seldom served. Usually three, or at most four, courses suffice for lunch or dinner; four or five for formal set dinner; two or three for supper; five or six for a banquet.

Hors d'oeuvre

This term applies to tangy, salty dishes to stimulate appetite; such as potato salad, anchovies, prawns, olives, Russian salad, Bismark herring, gendarmes, sardines, cold egg dishes; or to single items served before the soup, like melon, caviar, oysters, smoked salmon, salami, sausage, smoked ham.

Soup (potage)

Two soups are usually featured on a table d'hôte dinner: one clear (consommé) and one thick (crème, velouté or purée). Only one is served with each meal. The clear soup is listed on menus first.

Pasta (Italian and other pastas) and Eggs

Pasta (e.g. spaghetti, gnocchi, nouilles) may be served as a preliminary course at luncheon, either in place of or following the soup course.

Egg dishes (en cocotte, sur le plat, brouillés (scrambled), omelettes, etc.) may similarly be featured at this point.

Egg or pasta dishes are usually taken in place of a fish course if hors d'oeuvre and/or soup have been chosen. They are seldom included on set dinner menus, but may be chosen from the à la carte by guests taking less formal meals.

Grill Room Specialities

Smoked Scotch Salmon £8.25
Home Made Potted Crab Marinaded in Madeira £4.75
Native Oysters (per half dozen) £10.25
Potted Shrimps £4.00
Pâté of Duck Savoy Grill £5.25
Peppered Melon Surprise £4.75
Gallantine of Chicken and Brocolis £4.75

***

Omelette "Arnold Bennett" £4.75

Turnip and Watercress Soup £3.25

Eggs Bénédictine £4.25

Mushroom and Mustard Soup £3.25

***

Dover Sole Grilled or Pan Fried £12.75
Turbot, Clam and Leek Pie £12.50
Grilled Salmon Trout Accompanied by Spinach Pancakes £12.75

***

MONDAY

Farmhouse Sausages, Creamed Potatoes and Fried Onions £6.50
Pot Roast Spring Chicken served with a Purée of Carrots and Parsnips £8.75

TUESDAY

Lancashire Hot Pot £9.75
Steak, Kidney and Oyster Pudding £10.25

WEDNESDAY

Shepherds Pie and Glazed Swedes £9.75
Roast Loin of Pork and Apple Seasoning £9.75

THURSDAY

Rolled Chicken and Bacon Pie £11.25
Roast Rib of Beef and Yorkshire Pudding £11.75

FRIDAY

Cassoulet of Lamb and Haricot Beans £9.75
Smoked Haddock and Sea Bass Pie £10.25

Pan Fried Liver cooked with Apples and Raisins £10.75
Grilled Fillet Steak in a Mushroom Glaze £12.75
Grilled Sirloin Steak £12.25
Mixed Grill £11.75

Ragoo of Veal Kidneys £11.25
Grilled Barnsley Chop £10.75
Lamb Cutlets £11.25
Lamb Kidneys and Bacon £8.50

Roast Saddle and Leg of Lamb £10.75

All main courses are accompanied by fresh market vegetables

***

Sweet Trolley £3.50

Rice Pudding £3.50

Savoy Grill Room Savoury £3.50

Peach "Nellie" Melba £3.50

Canapé Baron £3.50

Keith R. Stanley, *Maître Chef de Cuisine*

Figure 4 Example of an à la carte luncheon menu, Grill Room, The Savoy.

Hors d'Oeuvres

Omelette au Crabe Othello £4.75
(Creamed Crab Meat Encased in a Savoury Omelette coated in a Tomatoed Vinaigrette)

Parfait de Gibier aux Truffes £5.75
(A Rich Game Pâté set on a strong Truffle and Madeira Dressing)

Jambon San Danièle et Grisson aux Figues £6.75
(Cured Ham and Swiss cured Beef served with sliced Figs)

Blinis et Deux Caviar £10.25
(Yeast Pancakes coated with a Soured Cream with Sevruga and Keeta Caviar)

Hors d'Oeuvres Chauds

Tasse d'Homard Parfumé au Fenouil £3.50
(Strong Lobster Bisque flavoured with Fennel)

Crème des Morilles aux Huîtres £3.75
(Wild Mushroom Velouté with Lettuce and Oysters)

Nouilles Verts à la Crème de Jambon £5.75
(Green Noodles bound with a Creamed Mushroom Sauce flavoured with Smoked Ham)

Poissons

Sole en Chevaux au Raifort £12.75
(Strips of Sole platted, steamed with Horseradish Cream with Lobster Essence)

St. Jacques Poêlé aux Piments Doux £12.25
(Scallops braised with sweet Peppers and a Pimento Bavaroise with Tarragon Essence)

Cassoulet d'Homard à l'Essence de Bois £21.25
(Sliced Lobster, Baby Vegetables and Wild Mushrooms cooked in White Wine Sauce served with Wild Rice)

Entrées

Suprême de Faisan aux Poivrons £12.25
*(Breast of Pheasant filled with a Puree of Morilles, cooked with
Red, Green and Yellow Peppers in a Tartlette case)*

Emincé de Boeuf Poché aux Capres £12.75
(Sliced Fillet of Poached Beef dressed on a Sharp Caper Sauce with Brocolis Flowers)

Gratin d'Agneau à la Mousse de Betterave £12.50
*(Lamb Cutlets coated with a Mousse of Beetroot, sauté with small
fritters of Spinach and Sweetcorn)*

Tous nos Poissons et Entrées sont Accompagnés d'un Légume ou d'une Garniture
(All Main Courses are served with Fresh Market Vegetables or Garnish)

Chariot du Pâtissier £3.50

Affinés du Maître Fromagier £3.50

***

Café Filtre £1.40   Café Espresso £1.40   Caffeine-Free Coffee £1.40

***

Prices are Inclusive of Service Charge and Value Added Tax   *Cover Charge £1.25*

Angelo Maresca, *Maître d'Hôtel*

Fish

Two kinds of fish are frequently offered on a table d'hôte dinner. One is invariably a poached fish served with a sauce mousseline or hollandaise or similar sauce. Plainly steamed or boiled potatoes are usually offered. (For luncheon the fish course can be replaced by a hot egg dish.)

Entrée

The entrée is the first of the meat courses. At dinner, usually, it is complete in itself, accompanied by its own vegetable or other garnish. It may be a dish like sweetbreads, garnished cutlets, vol au vent, liver, etc. (A luncheon entrée may be more substantial with additional vegetables served separately.)

Remove or relevé

This is a larger joint or 'pièce de resistance', for example a saddle of lamb, a cushion of veal, braised ham or even venison. Potatoes and one or two vegetables are served with this course.

The sorbet

The sorbet is a pause during a long meal, supposed to 'settle' dishes served and stimulate the appetite. It is a water ice, usually flavoured with champagne or some other delicate wine or liqueur and is served in a tall, small glass with a teaspoon. Cigarettes, usually Russian, are also passed and 10 minutes are allowed before the next course.

The roast (rôt)

Poultry or game, such as chicken, duck, turkey, pheasant, grouse or partridge, served with their sauces and gravy. A dressed salad is served separately on a half-moon plate. For shorter dinners (i.e. without an entrée) a fine meat roast such as a fillet of beef may be served.

Vegetables (legumes)

The French serve a finely dressed vegetable as a separate course, for example asparagus served with sauce hollandaise or beurre fondu. However, at lunch time (or even at a simple dinner) some choose this type of dish, that is globe artichokes or asparagus, as a preliminary course.

Sweet (entremet sucré)

This may consist of a hot sweet such as a soufflé or rum omelet, otherwise an ice (such as coupe, biscuit glacé, bombe glacée or meringue glacée). Petits fours (friandises or mignardises) are passed.

Savoury

A tit-bit on a hot canapé of toast or fried bread, or a hot soufflé (of, say, cheese or haddock) or a dainty savoury flan or ramequin.

Alternatively, the cheese platter (particularly at luncheon) may be presented; with biscuits, butter, celery, or watercress as probable accompaniments.

Dessert

This finale consists of a basket of fresh fruit (possibly also dried fruits and nuts). This is sometimes placed on the table as part of the decorations.

Finally, coffee is served and liqueurs and brandy passed.

Menu balance

A suitable menu conforms to:

- principles of digestibility
- customer's individual preferences
- season of the year and nature of the occasion
- resources of kitchen staff and equipment (what it is possible to prepare in the time)
- cost and price policy
- not only nutritional and digestive balance but also varied flavour, colour, texture and consistency

Regular menus are normally composed by the chef (or caterer) in accordance with the management's policy; however, a menu for a pre-ordered party will usually be compiled by the restaurant manager in consultation with the chef. The former should know what customers desire and the chef what can be prepared by his staff on the day in question and within the costs allowed.

Factors in menu composition

It is useless to compile a menu which could be prepared only with more kitchen staff than exist or which demand more skill than is possessed by the chef and his assistants. There is a difference between compiling a menu for a busy restaurant which has to serve to capacity and at a high speed during rush hours and one for a leisurely banquet.

The following should be considered when compiling a menu.

- Avoid two dishes composed of the same ingredients, for example if an egg dish is on the menu then eggs should not form part of the hors d'oeuvre; if the soup is Crème Dubarry (which contains cauliflower as its base) do not serve cauliflower later as a vegetable. If pie or pastry is served, for example vol au vent, do not serve any starchy food, for example apple pie, as sweet

- Two white meats or two dark meats should never follow each other, for example pork should not be followed by veal nor beef by mutton. (There are so many different dishes that this duplication can easily be avoided.)
- Follow a light entrée by a heavier dish
- If the menu is long, choose dishes that are not so heavy; for example, for a big banquet earlier dishes should be without bulk
- If the menu is short, possibly include dishes which have consistency or bulk to ensure that diners will have sufficient

The two menu types

There are two main kinds of menu; à la carte and table d'hôte. The former lists all the dishes within the resources of the restaurant's kitchen (see Figures 3 and 4) and from which the guest selects his own menu. The table d'hôte (literally and originally the 'host's' or hoteliers own table) is a meal at a fixed price with limited or no choice (Figures 5 and 6). The waiter may be asked for guidance in the guest's choice from both kinds of menu.

The Dorchester

LUNCHEON MENU

Avocat Vichysoisse Froid
(Cold Vichysoisse Soup flavoured with Avocado)

* * *

Mignons d'Agneau aux Betterave
(Boned Lamb Cutlets sautéed with Beetroot)
Pommes au Thym
(Potatoes roasted with Thyme)
Légume du Marché
(Fresh Market Vegetable)

* * *

Gratin aux Fruits de la Saison
(Sliced Fruits glazed in Crème Caramel)

* * *

Café
Petits Fours

285 LB

Figure 5   Exmple of a table d'hôte luncheon menu, The Dorchester.

PRE-THEATRE

Two Courses . . . £15.00
including Coffee

La Tasse de Homard Fenouillette
A light lobster soup flavoured with brandy and fennel

Le Jambon de Parme aux Figues
Smoked parma ham with sliced figs

La Mousseline des Légumes Homardine
Vegetable mousse with a lobster dressing and seafood

Les Filets de Sole au Xérès
Fillets of sole cooked with sherry and mushrooms

L'Emincé de Veau à l'Auberge de Bois
Sliced loin of veal cooked with wild mushrooms and sage

La Selle d'Agneau Rôtie
Roast saddle of lamb with garnish of the day

Le Plat du Jour
Choice from today's trolley

Les Entremets de la Voiture
Les Fromages au Choix
Les Glacés Variés, Gaufrettes Roulées

Le Café
Expresso, Filter, Hag

Available from 18.00 – 19.15 hrs

PRE AND AFTER THEATRE

Three Courses . . . £25.00
including Coffee

If you wish
First and Main Courses before the Theatre.
Return after the Show and relax with
Dessert and Coffee.

La Salade de Foie Blond au Xérès
Strips of liver cooked with sherry vinegar on seasonal salads

Le Saumon d'Ecosse Fumé
Scotch smoked salmon

La Timbale de Melon aux Poivres
Delicate melon cocktail with a creamed peppercorn dressing

La Velouté des Champignons au Moutarde
Cream of mushroom soup flavoured with mustard

Le Zephir de Truite Saumonée aux Crêpes d'Epinards
Salmon trout grilled with a tomato purée and spinach pancakes

La Mousseline de Saumon Fumé en Croûte aux Ciboulettes
A light smoked salmon mousse cooked in pastry with chives

L'Aiguillettes de Volaille Poché aux Truffes
Sliced breast of chicken poached in a truffle sauce with wild rice

La Selle d'Agneau Rôtie
Roast Saddle of lamb with garnish of the day

Le Plat du Jour
Choice from today's trolley

Le Chariot du Patisseur
Les Affinés du Maître Fromagier
Les Sorbets Variés, Biscuits sec

Le Café
Expresso, Filter, Hag

Prices include Value Added Tax and Service Charge

Figure 6 Example of a table d'hôte theatre menu, The Savoy.

Be familiar with all the dishes and their composition and memorize them; and appreciate the fundamentals of blending courses to help compose an acceptable suggestion. Finally, to comprehend and then be able to explain to customers French expressions on a menu, make yourself familiar with the words for food and methods of cookery listed earlier, and note the basic menu language in Chapter 4.

4
Product Knowledge III: Menu Terms

Most menus in Britain and America today are written in English and this is sensible when dishes and their range are of our own tradition. Even when menus are written in French, many establishments add an English translation or interpretation. Nevertheless a waiter may still encounter a French menu or French terms on a menu and this chapter is intended to provide a basis for menu understanding.

Menu names for food

In the following lists, course by course, the food, commodity or cut is named. Examples of styles or garnishes are then listed.

Hors d'oeuvre

Hors d'oeuvre items

Anchois	Anchovies
Anguille fumée	Smoked eel
Artichauts (fonds d'artichauts)	Globe artichokes (artichoke bottoms)
Betterave	Beetroot
Céleri-rave	Celeriac
Champignons	Mushrooms
Charcuterie	Cold sausage, smoked ham, etc.
Crevettes grises	Shrimps
Crevettes roses	Prawns
Escargots	Snails
Huitres	Oysters
Jambon	Ham
Jambon de Bayonne, de Parme	Bayonne ham and Parma ham (varieties of smoked ham
Pamplemousse	Grapefruit

Pâté	Paste or potted meat or fish, hence pâté de foie gras, goose liver paste or pâté maison, pâté in 'the style of the house'
Radis	Radishes
Riz	Rice
Saucisson	Cold sausage
Salami	Italian variety of sausage
Saumon fumé	Smoked salmon
Thon	Tunny fish
Tomates	Tomatoes
Truite fumé	Smoked trout

Hors d'oeuvre terms

à l'huile	With oil
Barquette	Boat-shaped pastry tartlette filled with savoury item (fish roe, mousse, etc.)
Bouchée	Small puff paste case with savoury filling
Canapé	Small bread slice, toasted, or fried, garnished with savoury item. Served hot or cold (also as savoury course when hot)
Carolines	Small savoury filled choux paste buns
Greque, à la	Greek style (i.e. rice with pimento, raisins)
Strasbourgeoise	Strasbourg style (for pâté de foie gras)

Soups

Soup items

Bisque	Thick soup, normally fish especially shell fish
Bortsch	Russian (or Polish) broth with sour cream, beetroot juice, pirogs (little dumplings)
Bouillabaisse	Stew-like fish soup from South of France
Bouillon	Broth
Chowder	American potato soup, normally incorporating fish
Consommé	Clear soup
Crème	Cream soup
Croûte	Crust
Croûte au pot	Clear soup garnished with croûtes
Croûtons	Sippets of fried bread
Fausse totue	Mock turtle

Minestrone	Italian, tomato-flavoured broth, garnished with vegetables, Italian paste. Accompaniment: grated Parmesan cheese
Petite Marmite	Small earthenware pot which gives its name to the clear, strong, garnished consommé served in it
Potage	Any thick soup
Pot-au-feu	French-style beef and bone broth with vegetable garnish
Soupe à l'oignon	Onion soup
Tortue	Turtle
Velouté	Alternative designation for cream soup
Waterzoi	A stew-like fish soup

Styles of soup

Bonne femme, potage	Leek and onion soup
Brunoise, consommé	Clear soup, garnished with finely diced vegetable
Célestine, consommé	Clear soup garnished with fine strips of pancake
Créçy, crème	Cream of carrot soup
Faubonne, crème	Butter bean soup
Jackson, crème	Cream of potato soup
Julienne, consommé	Clear soup, garnished with fine strips of vegetables
Palestine, crème	Cream of Jerusalem artichoke
Parmentier, potage	Potato soup
Princesse, velouté	Cream of chicken soup
Vichyssoise	Cold cream potato soup, with chopped chives

Italian paste (pasta) and rice (Figure 7)

Italian paste and rice items

Canneloni	Stuffed type of Italian paste
Fettucine	Strip-type Italian paste
Lasagne	Italian noodle
Gnocchi	A small paste 'dumpling' of semolina (Italian) or chou paste (French) or potato paste
Macaroni	Tubular form of Italian paste
Nouilles	Noodles

Spaghetti	Finer tubular form of Italian paste
Pilaff	Rice, usually cooked in stock with light garnish
Ravioli	Stuffed form of Italian pasta
Riz	Rice
Risotto	Cooked rice dish, usually garnished
Tagliatelli	An Italian pasta

Figure 7   Different types of pasta.

Pasta and rice styles

Bolognaise	With minced meat sauce
Italienne	Dressed with butter and grated cheese
Milanaise	With tomato sauce, julienne of ham and tongue
Napolitaine	With tomato sauce and grated Parmesan cheese
Parmesan, au	With Parmesan cheese

Eggs

Types of cooked egg (oeuf)

à la coque	Soft boiled in shell
Cocotte, en	Baked and served in small fireproof dish
Brouillés	Scrambled
Dur	Hard boiled
Mollet	Soft boiled without shell
Omelette	Omelet
Sur le plat	Baked and served in same dish

Egg styles

à la reine	En cocotte with cream and diced chicken
Argenteuil	Soft boiled, shelled with creamed sauce and asparagus tips (Argenteuil denotes asparagus)
Berçy	Sur le plat, with grilled chipolata sausages, tomato sauce
Chasseur	Sur le plat, with chicken liver and chasseur sauce (*q.v.*)
Chimay	Hard boiled, duxelle stuffed, coated with Mornay sauce and glazed
Florentine	On spinach, coated with Mornay sauce and glazed

Omelet garnishes

Aux fines herbes	With chopped herbs (usually parsley predominates)
Aux champignons	Mushrooms
Aux rognons	Kidney
Clamart	Stuffed with peas à la française
Espagnole	Spanish omelette (served plate-shaped, flat) with onion, tomato, pimento. Garnish, half-stone olive and anchovy strips

Fish

Fish and their cuts

Barbue	Brill
Blanchaille	Whitebait
Brandade	Dish of salt cod
Coquille St Jacques	Scallop

Côtelette	Cutlet (alternative term for tronçon (*q.v.*))
Darne	Finest straight cut through middle (usually of salmon and similar large fish) with bone
Filet	Fillet
Fruits de mer	Literally 'sea fruit', usually denotes shell fish
Homard	Lobster
Laitance	Soft herring roe
Langouste	Crawfish, spiny lobster
Limande	Lemon sole
Merlan	Whiting
Mignon	Fillet of sole (or similar fish) in triangular fold as cornet
Morue	Salt cod
Moules	Mussels
Paupiette	Fillet (of sole or similar) flattened, stuffed and rolled
Plie	Place
Rouget	Red mullet
Scampi	Dublin Bay prawns
Sole de Douvres	Dover sole
Suprème	Alternative term for fillet
Tronçon	Steak cut of fish with bone

Fish styles

à l'Anglaise	Egg and crumbed and deep fried
Au beurre noir	With black butter
Au beurre noisette	With butter heated to nutty stage
Au bleu	Poaching live trout, giving skin a blue tinge
Carapace, en	(Of lobsters) in the shell
Colbert (sole)	Sole slit on one side, with fillets then folded back; crumbed, deep fried and maître d'hôtel butter placed in slit
Colère, en	For whiting, head affixed to tail, deep fried
Coulibiac, (de saumon)	Special dish of salmon cooked in paste
Bonne femme	In velouté sauce with mushrooms
Dugléré	With white wine sauce, tomato
Goujons, en	In strips (for frying or meunière)
Maître d'hôtel	With maitre d'hotel butter (lemon, parsley butter)

Otéro	Served in half, baked potato on shell fish garnish with mornay sauce coating
Newburg	For shell fish (usually lobster pieces). Tossed in butter, flamed in brandy, covered with cream and egg yolk. Garnish, truffle. Serve with pilaff rice
Thermidor	For lobster. Served in mustard flavoured, cheese sauce in the half shell
Véronique	Velouté sauce, garnished with peeled grapes
Vin blanc (sole, etc.)	In white wine sauce

Meat course

Meat, game and poultry items

Butcher's meat

Agneau	Lamb
Agneau, carré d'	Best end of lamb
Agneau, côtelette d'	Cutlet
Agneau, gigot d'	Leg of lamb
Agneau, noisette d'	Boneless small cut equivalent to boned loin chop or cutlet
Agneau, selle d'	Saddle of lamb
Andouille, andouillette	Sausage of pork chitterling type
Baron, of beef	Double sirloin
Baron of mutton (or lamb)	Saddle with legs attached
Bifteck	Steak
Bitok	Minced meat, shaped as tournedos
Blanquette	White stew of white meat
Boeuf	Beef
Boeuf, aloyau de	Sirloin, with bone
Boeuf, côte de	Rib
Boeuf, filet de	Fillet of beef
Boudin, blanc	White pudding (white sausage)
Boudin, noir	Black pudding (blood sausage)
Carbonnade de boeuf	Stewed steak with beer as ingredient
Cassoulet	Braised meats (usually pork, goose or sausage) with haricot beans
Coeur	Heart. Describes dainty cut of fillet beef, for example coeur de filet
Côte à l'os	Rib cut beef steak (equivalent to a large cutlet)

Carpetbag steak	Large steak (usually double entrecôte) split, stuffed with oysters and sewn
Cervelle	Brain
Châteaubriand	Double portion steak cut from 'head' or thick end of beef fillet
Entrecôte	Sirloin steak
Entrecôte minute	Thin, flattened entrecôte steak
Escalope	Thin collop of meat, usually veal or pork
Filet mignon	Fillet from saddle of lamb or mutton
Foie	Liver
Fricassé	White stew of white meat or chicken
Hanche de venaison	Haunch of venison (half saddle with leg attached)
Jambon	Ham
Langue	Tongue
Médaillon	Medallion, name for smaller collop of meat such as veal or pork
Mouton	Mutton (see agneau for cuts and joints)
Navarin	Brown stew of lamb or mutton
Porc	Pork
Porc, cuisse or cuissot de	Leg of pork
Porc, longe de	Loin of pork
Porc, pieds de	Pork trotters
Porterhouse steak	'T' bone (prime sirloin steak on bone) from the large end of the loin
Pré salé	Mutton or lamb raised on pasture near sea
Queue de boeuf	Oxtail
Ragout	Rich and well-seasoned stew
Rognons	Kidneys
Rognonnade de veau	Saddle of veal complete with kidneys
Saucisse	Sausage
Rosbif	Roast beef
Tête de veau	Calf's head
Tournedos	Small round, fillet steak
Venaison	Venison

Poultry and small game

Canard	Duck
Caneton	Duckling
Civet de lièvre	Jugged hare
Cuisse de poulet	Leg of chicken
Crapaudine	Split whole (spatchcock) chicken, grilled and dressed to resemble a toad
Dindonneau	Young turkey

Gibier	Game
Lapin	Rabbit
Lapereau	Young hare
Perdreau, perdrix	Partridge
Pintade	Guinea fowl
Poussin	Chick
Salmis	Stew of game
Volaille	Fowl

Main course styles and garnishes

Alsacienne	With sauerkraut
Américaine	With grills – bacon, tomato, straw potatoes
Bouquetière	With mixed vegetables, turned (i.e. shaped) into small olives
Bourgeoise	(With braises) turned carrots, lardons and button onions
Clamart	With peas, for example artichoke bottoms stuffed with purée of peas with château potatoes
Dubarry	Denotes cauliflower with, say, noisettes of lamb – cauliflower topped with Mornay and sauce Madère
Holstein	Breadcrumbed veal escalope: fried egg, lemon sliver, anchovy fillets
Maryland	Segmented fried chicken (egg and crumbed) with banana fritters, sweetcorn pancake, tomato, bacon, croquette potato, horseradish cream
Niçoise	With French beans, tomato, château potatoes
Polonaise	For poussin, stuffed and poêlé, topped with chopped egg, buttered breadcrumbs
Printanière	With mixed, spring vegetable garnish
Provençale	With a gravy of meat stock, herbs, shallots, mushrooms and garlic
Rossini	With tournedos, topping of foie gras collop, truffle slice and Madeira sauce
Soissonnaise	(For braises) with haricot beans
King, chicken, à la	Diced chicken in cream sauce
Moussaka	A Balkan dish of aubergines stuffed with minced lamb

Garnishes

Note that among garnishes some are:

- decorative but not meant to be eaten, for example socles, butter and ice carving
- decorative but edible, for example parsley, watercress
- edible and part of the dish, for example vegetables, sauce, fruits

Vegetables (legumes)

Aubergine	Egg plant
Boutons de Bruxelles	Tiny Brussels sprouts
Carottes	Carrots
Champignons	Mushrooms
Chou	Cabbage
Choucroûte	Sauerkraut
Chou de mer	Seakale
Choufleur	Cauliflower
Courge (courgette)	Vegetable marrow (young marrow)
Cresson	Watercress
Epinards	Spinach
Flageolets	Kidney beans
Laitue	Lettuce
Macédoine de legumes	Diced mixed vegetables
Navet	Turnips
Navet de Suede	Swedes
Oignons	Onions
Poireaux	Leeks
Pommes de terres	Potatoes (see below for modes of serving). Usually abbreviated to pommes, for example pommes château
Salsifis	Salsify

Potato styles

There are numerous methods of cooking potatoes, some of which are listed below.

Allumettes	Match size, deep fried
Anna	Sliced, pressed and baked in mould
Au four	Jacket baked. Cut with cross incision before service
Boulangère	Sliced, with sliced onion, stock moistened and baked
Château	Turned to olive size, blanched then roasted in butter

Duchesse	Purée with egg yolk, then piped through forcing bag
En purée	Mashed
En robe de chambre	Boiled or steamed in jacket
En robe de champs	Alternative designation (literally in field dress) for en robe de chambre
Fondantes	Large egg shaped, cooked in butter and stock with upper surface thus glazed
Frites	Deep fried or 'French' fried
Gaufrettes	Lattice-cut, deep fried
Lyonnaise	Sautées with onions
Nature	Plain boiled
Persillées	Steamed or boiled potatoes, tossed in butter with chopped parsley
Rissolées	Browned in fat
Soufflées	Rectangular slices deep fried twice in order to 'balloon' them
Vapeur	Turned to 'château' (*q.v.*) size and steamed.

Styles for other vegetables

Au beurre fondu	With melted butter
à la moêlle	With poached beef-bone marrow
Farçis	Stuffed, for example tomatoes, artichoke bottoms, etc. (usually with duxelle)
Vichy	Carrots cooked in Vichy water and butter until completely evaporated and glazed

Fruits

Abricot	Apricot
Ananas	Pineapple
Canteloupe	Type of melon
Citron	Lemon
Fraises du bois (alt. Fraises des bois)	Wood or wild strawberries
Pêche	Peach
Poire	Pear
Pomme	Apple
Raisin	Grape
Reine Claude	Greengage
Tutti frutti	Italian term for mixed, candied fruits (usually chopped) often served in or with ice cream

Sweet and dessert items

Au Kirsch	With Kirsch liqueur
Baba au rhum	Yeast leavened light sponge soaked in rum
Bande de fruits	Long, narrow type of fruit flan
Bavarois	Bavarian cream; a cream and egg dessert set with gelatine
Beignet	Fritter
Bombe (glacée)	Bomb or shell shaped ice
Chantilly	Whipped and lightly sweetened fresh cream
Compôte	Stewed fruit, hence compôte d'abricots (stewed apricots)
Coupe	Silver or glass, stemmed dish for ice cream dishes
Crème	Cream
Crème au chocolat	Chocolate cream
Crêpe	Pancake
Eclair	Choux pastry filled with cream or crème pâtissier
Gâteau	Cake
Marrons glacés	Chestnuts glazed by boiling in syrup
Meringues (glacées)	Sugar and egg white confection (with ice cream)
Millefeuilles, gâteau	Gâteau of puff paste
Melba, sauce	Raspberry purée sauce. Hence pêche or pear Melba (the fruit served with ice cream, Melba sauce and cream)
Nesselrode	Denotes chestnuts
Poire Hélène	Pear on ice cream with hot chocolate sauce
Panachées	Mixed, for example glaces panachées, ices of mixed colours and flavours
Pâtisseries	Pastries
Tarte	Tart
Savarin	Similar mix to Baba but shaped as hollow ring
Suchard	Denotes chocolate
Singapore	Denotes pineapple

Common sauces

The selection below indicates principal characteristics of sauces commonly served with meats, fish, poultry and vegetables.

Aioli	Mayonnaise (*q.v.*) with garlic

Allemande	Reduced velouté (*q.v.*) with liaison of egg yolk
Américaine	Tomato sauce blended with lobster butter
Anchois	Cream sauce, anchovy flavoured
Aurore	Velouté or Béchamel (*q.v.*) tinted and flavoured with tomato
Béarnaise	Hollandaise (*q.v.*) with chopped tarragon
Béarnaise brune	As above tinted with meat glaze
Béchamel	A thick white sauce of milk, flour and butter
Berçy	Thick brown stock, white wine, chopped shallots and fines herbes
Bordelaise	Red wine, half glaze, marrow, chopped shallots. Served mostly with red meat
Biggarade	Demi-glace (*q.v.*) with julienne of orange zest, orange juice
Champignons	White or brown sauce with mushrooms
Charcutière	Robert (*q.v.*) with sliced gherkin garnish
Chasseur	White wine sauce reduced with concassé (chopped and de-pipped) tomatoes and sliced mushrooms
Choron	Tomato flavoured hollandaise (*q.v.*)
Demi-glace	Half glaze, that is thickened brown stock (Espagnole) reduced
Diable	Reduction of wine vinegar, wine, chopped shallots with demi-glace (*q.v.*) well seasoned with cayenne
Duxelle	A thick sauce (virtually a stuffing) of chopped mushrooms and shallots moistened with wine and demi-glace
Financière	Madeira sauce (sauce madère, *q.v.*) with chicken essence, mushrooms (and, sometimes, truffles)
Grand veneur	Poivrade (*q.v.*) and Espagnole with game blood and essense
Gribiche	Thin mayonnaise with fines herbes
Hollandaise	Emulsion of eggs, butter, lemon – warm
Lyonnaise	Cooked, sliced onions in cream sauce (usually) or brown sauce
Madère	Demi-glace flavoured with Madeira wine
Maître d'hôtel	(a) Hard slice of butter with lemon juice and chopped parsley (b) Velouté (*q.v.*) richened with maître d'hôtel butter

Marchand de vins	Red wine brown sauce with chopped shallots
Marinière	White wine fish sauce with fines herbes
Matelote	As Bordelaise with fish glaze and anchovy flavouring in place of meat glaze
Mayonnaise	Emulsion of eggs, oil, vinegar and mustard – cold
Mornay	Béchamel (*q.v.*) with grated cheese
Mousseline	Hollandaise (*q.v.*) with whipped cream
Newburg	Butter, cream, yolks of eggs, sherry
Périgueux	Madère (*q.v.*) with truffles
Piquante	Tomaté half glaze, with vinegar reduction and gherkin garnish
Poivrade	As piquante (*q.v.*) but without gherkin
Portugaise	Tomato with onion, garlic flavour
Poulette	Velouté (*q.v.*) with egg yolk liaison, mushroom essence and lemon juice finish
Raifort	Cream sauce with horseradish
Ravigote	Egg yolks, oil, vinegar and chopped herbs
Reform	Madère (*q.v.*) with julienne of egg white, cooked tongue and truffle
Robert	Demi-glace (*q.v.*) with white wine, sliced onion flavour
Soubise	Thick white sauce of onion and cream
Tartare	Mayonnaise with chopped gherkins, capers, gherkins, capers, fines herbes – cold
Verte	Mayonnaise with fines herbes and green colouring

Further common menu terms

To interpret a French menu or understand restaurant jargon, the reader should also be familiar with other words, such as the examples given below.

à la	After the style, or fashion of, for example: à la française, French style; à la russe, Russian style. Also with (or dressed in), for example à la crème, with or in cream
à la carte	On the menu (literally card): implies many dishes at different prices for the guest's choice. Normally cooked to order (as distinct from table d'hôte, *q.v.*)

au	Masculine form of à la (*q.v.*)
Biscotte	Rusk
Café	Coffee
Café au lait	Coffee with milk
Café double	Double strength coffee for lunch and dinner
Café noir	Coffee without cream or milk, that is black coffee
Carte du jour	Menu of the day
Chauffe-plats	Sideboard hot plates
Couvert	Cover or place setting
Déjeuner	Lunch
Demi-tasse	Literally, half cup, small coffee cup
Diner	Dinner
Entrée	A composed, garnished dish served before the roast or main meat course (or, at luncheon, served as main course)
Entremet	Sweet course (formerly entremet sucré; as an entremet de legume, separate vegetable course, was equally frequently served)
Fromage	Cheese
Guéridon	Side-table (for service); nowadays may be a wheeled table or cart
Mise en place	Literally 'put in place'. To waiters implies pre-preparation of sideboards, table, restaurant, etc.
Petit déjeuner	Breakfast
Plat du jour	Special dish of the day
Réchaud	'Lamp' or small spirit stove for restaurant re-heating or cooking
Souper	Supper
Table d'hôte	A set meal, usually of several courses, at a fixed, inclusive price
Timbale	A round deep dish of straight sides
Vol au vent	Puff pastry case usually filled with diced chicken, fish, etc. dressed in sauce
Voiture	Carriage or trolley for example for hors d'oeuvre or pastries
Wagon	Alternative name for voiture

5
Waiting Tasks and Titles

Waiting staff organization is affected by factors like the type of customer sought and prices to be charged. The food and beverage served also affects waiting procedures and staff. Large, traditionally staffed cuisines involved a large brigade of waiters.

In a book about waiting, emphasis is inevitable on establishments which *employ* waiting staff. But operations where waiting skills are not used or are minimal are also important. The massive market for fast food for eaters-out demonstrates its economic and social significance. However, where waiter's skills effect or aid sales they are vital; and it must be remembered that skills may be modified to meet simple requirements. For example, a salad or a baked potato may be dressed from a side table without staff having to master the whole range of guéridon skills.

Waiting staff are interested in the hierarchy of an old style French restaurant brigade from commis to maître d'hôtel, because between the two wars there was little change in staffing in restaurants employing waiters. The tradition is shown in Figure 8. However, in recent years change in service requirements has affected staff patterns. Many traditional subdivisions of tasks are meaningless as old styles of service disappear.

Awareness of traditional grades of staff and service helps in understanding waiting development, but waiting constantly adapts to new requirements. Management assesses the nature of the work, groups tasks to enable that work to be done effectively and need not be concerned by 'traditional' patterns when deciding on numbers of posts. For example, preliminary work in cleaning the restaurant may now be done by domestic staff; although some cleaning or ménage may remain for waiters.

Nature of tasks

Apart from 'selling' and the cleaning (or ménage) already mentioned, waiting staff duties involve:

- preparing restaurant, sideboards and tables
- greeting customers

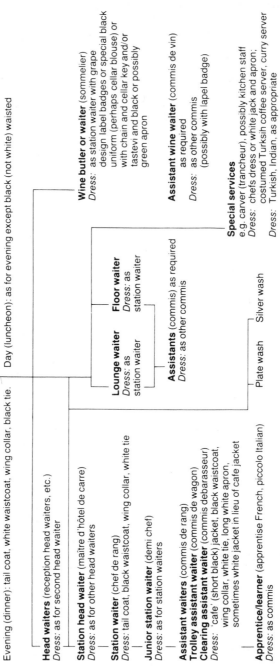

Figure 8   Staff and dress of an old-style French restaurant.

Restaurant manager or head waiter (maître d'hôtel)

Dress: * Day: morning suit (black jacket, short or long), striped trousers.   * Evening: white tie and tails or dinner jacket

Assistant or second head waiter

Evening (dinner): tail coat, white waistcoat, wing collar, black tie.   Day (luncheon): as for evening except black (not white) waisted

Wine butler or waiter (sommelier)
Dress: as station waiter with grape design label badges or special black uniform (perhaps cellar blouse) or with chain and cellar key and/or tastevi and black or possibly green apron

Assistant wine waiter (commis de vin) as required
Dress: as other commis (possibly with lapel badge)

Special services
e.g. carver (trancheur), possibly kitchen staff
Dress: chefs dress or white jack and apron; costumed Turkish coffee server, curry server
Dress: Turkish, Indian, as appropriate

Head waiters (reception head waiters, etc.)
Dress: as for second head waiter

Station head waiter (maître d'hôtel de carre)
Dress: as for other head waiters

Station waiter (chef de rang)
Dress: tail coat, black waistcoat, wing collar, white tie

Junior station waiter (demi chef)
Dress: as for station waiters

Assistant waiters (commis de rang)
Trolley assistant waiter (commis de wagon)
Clearing assistant waiter (commis debarasseur)
Dress: 'cafe' (short black) jacket, black waistcoat, wing collar, white tie, long white apron, sometimes white jacket in lieu of cafe jacket

Apprentice/learner (apprentise French, piccolo Italian)
Dress: as commis

If restaurant manager, otherwise dress as for other head waiters.

Lounge waiter
Dress: as station waiter

Floor waiter
Dress: as station waiter

Assistants (commis) as required
Dress: as other commis

Plate wash   Silver wash

Dress notes:

* If restaurant manager, otherwise dress as for other head waiters.
1. Waitresses: traditionally wore black (or dark) dress, washable collars, cuffs and cap (all usually white), stockings and simple black shoes.
2. Modern style: regarding today's approach to uniform for men and women.

- serving food
- serving beverages
- clearing tables, sideboards
- presenting bills and bidding farewell

Procedures which these tasks require are introduced in the chapters which follow. Figure 8 indicates how restaurant practices have become formalized with tasks identified with named staff. Even today, some waiting staff may specialize, that is become wine butlers or wine waiters and others rise to maîtres d'hôtel.

Supervising tasks

Traditionally the restaurant manager (directeur du restaurant) was responsible for all the restaurant service and took charge of all those connected with it. He quoted prices for daily menus and, in addition (unless there was a separate banqueting manager), made arrangements for banquets and private parties.

The head waiter (maître d'hôtel) took charge of either the whole of a small restaurant or part of a larger one. He supervised service, received guests (either directly or from the restaurant manager) and seated them. He might take orders from guests and pass them to station waiters. In large establishments there might be subordinate or assistant head waiters, that is second or third head waiters (deuxième or troisième maîtres d'hôtel) and/or in a sufficiently large establishment a reception head waiter (maître d'hôtel de reception) to maintain a room plan of numbered tables, take telephone bookings, enter them in a reservation book and later receive guests and direct them to a table.

Stations or groups of tables would be grouped further under a station head waiter (maître d'hôtel de carré) who was responsible in his section of the restaurant for duties similar to those of the maître d'hôtel.

Most of these duties still have to be carried out; though how they are allocated and titled nowadays may vary from the old-style pattern.

Greeting

Senior staff (such as those noted above) are prominently involved in greeting customers; though all waiters will do so when guests arrive at their station or tables.

Serving

In serving meals the traditional 'restaurant brigade' arrangement was for a station waiter (chef de rang) to take charge of a 'rang' or group of about five tables to seat approximately 20 guests. A chef de rang normally had an assistant waiter (commis de rang) or he might be a single-handed waiter (demi chef) working without an assistant.

In serving beverages, however, the task is often still allocated to a specialist wine butler or waiter (sommelier) who may have a younger waiter to assist him (commis de vin).

Clearing and assisting

Clearing tables and sideboards involved the most junior assistant as clearing waiter (commis débarrasseur), 'fetching and carrying' (usually clearing away) under instructions.

Commis

Several kinds of junior assistants are known as commis. Duties of the assistant station waiter (commis de rang; also known as commis de suite) include:

- pass food checks to the kitchen
- bring dishes to sidetables
- remove plates from guests' tables
- return used plates and dishes to the service area
- generally attend on the station

A trolley assistant waiter (commis de wagon) is assigned to a trolley (a voiture or wagon) usually of hors d'oeuvres or pâtisserie.

In apprenticeship, young waiters (apprentis) work up through the assistant posts. In continental brigades such youngsters were called piccolos (literally 'little ones' from the Italian).

Commis duties

In restaurants where there are still commis (assistant waiters), they should do more than merely act on the instructions of a chef de rang. They should be unobtrusively helpful at all stages, for example, assisting when necessary (i.e. absence of more senior staff or with larger parties when more than one waiter is needed) in guest seating and such tasks as unfolding napkins, distributing menus, placing bread and butter and filling water glasses when parties arrive.

During service commis:

- bring required dishes from servery to station sideboard (looking at order checks on the sideboard so that they learn to anticipate the chef de rang's requirements). They must understand procedures in ordering on the servery
- clear tables of used items such as plates, glasses and unwanted cutlery and other items and clear sideboards
- replenish sideboards with needed cutlery, crockery, etc. so that there is enough equipment to meet all requirements

- empty and change ashtrays
- attend to guests' water glasses
- clear and re-lay tables when vacated in readiness for re-seating. When table cloth is soiled, change and immediately re-set covers, replacing cruets, flowers and clean ashtray
- ensure neatness of the rang, that is remove crumbs from chairs, pick up waste from floor, remove empty cigarette packets and match boxes

Other staff

In addition, there were, and still are, waiters who work outside the restaurant serving teas, beverages, etc. in the lounges (lounge waiters), breakfasts and other meals and beverages on the floors (floor waiters), as well as barmen or American barmen and carvers (trancheurs) who work either from a buffet or trolley.

Additionally, restaurants may employ specialist staff such as costumed Turkish coffee or Indian curry servers.

Presenting bills and the cashier

Procedures for presenting the bill to a customer are outlined in Chapter 19. Sometimes the waiter makes out the bill and sometimes it is the responsibility of a cashier, either at a cash desk in the restaurant itself or in the service area.

6
Dress, Hygiene and Behaviour

Grades of seniority of waiters are customarily indicated by variations in waiting uniform. Originally this derived from evening dress (see Figure 8).

Just as traditional tasks and categories of staff have little relevance today, so does traditional dress; but staff are usually required by management to wear some kind of uniform often designed to fit a theme.

Practical clothing (Figure 9)

Washable clothing which can be changed daily or for each meal as may be required is preferred. Conventional operations favour white jackets with patrol type collars, not requiring collars and tie or jackets which look smart when worn with turn-down collars. Detachable epaulettes and/or lapel facings may be used to 'smarten' or give 'character' to jackets.

Waiting dress should:

- be comfortable, practical
- allow free movement
- be hygienic
- look good to both guest and the waiter himself
- blend with and contribute to a restaurant's ambience
- have strong pockets to withstand use of order pads, bottle openers, cash, etc.

Head dress

Caps or head bands are no longer universally worn by waitresses who should, however, adopt simple, short hair styles.

Guide to quantity of clothing

There are no rigid rules for quantity but the following would suffice per person in a conventional restaurant:

Figure 9 Practical dress for a waiter and waitress.

Waiters
Four washable patrol type jackets
One set of buttons (plus epaulettes and facings according to 'house' style)
Two pairs of trousers (often black 'evening' style without turn-ups)
Four pairs of plain, black socks

Waitresses
Two uniform dresses (black no longer universal)
Four aprons (usually bibbed)
Four sets of cuffs (usually white for wrist or upperarm if half-sleeve dresses)
Four headbands or caps (if worn)
Two pairs of plain shoes (black, court style, medium heels suggested)
Four pairs of stockings/tights

Waiters and waitresses
Underclothing: four complete sets at least to ensure adequate change.
Additionally, service cloths are supplied for each meal service.
    In old fashioned operations commis waiters were provided with white
aprons.

Changing and the locker room

Use the changing and locker rooms for their proper purpose and use the appropriate accommodation for leisure recreation.

- Help maintain your locker and changing room tidy and clean
- Keep all your belongings in your own locker
- Put clothing away carefully and do not leave lying about
- Ensure your lockers lock; and keep them locked
- Put unwanted paper, cloths, cigarette ends in the proper receptacles

Care of dress

Your appearance helps to sell an establishment's service and food; and you yourself. First impressions count a great deal to guests (and to your boss).

- Be smart on arriving for restaurant duty
- Never appear before the public unless in full uniform
- Change fully in the dressing room. (Waitresses should never, for example, put on aprons 'in the room')
- Observe cleanliness in dress, particularly cuffs, aprons, collars, etc. (Remember, bacteria may spread by dirty clothes coming into contact with food or implements)

Dress issued

Regulations differ between restaurants in regard to changing and charging for clothing. A waiter is usually responsible for the supply and upkeep of his clothing, but many hotels and restaurants arrange, at the establishment's cost, for laundering waiters' linen. For example, some may supply and/or launder jackets at no cost to waiters.

A waiter may receive one (or more) jacket(s) (plus a set of house buttons, epaulettes or trimmings) as a basic issue to be changed for clean as authorized. When he leaves, final pay is withheld until this (and any other company property) is returned. In default, its value may be deducted from any pay due.

Personal clothing

Apart from 'house' issues, ensure that you have:

Underclothing   An adequate supply to ensure frequent washing. Waiting involves movement in a warm atmosphere; daily change of vest and underpants for men (and similar underwear for waitresses) avoids the risk of garments smelling.

Socks, stockings and tights Again, an adequate quantity for frequent (at least daily) change of socks (waiters) and stockings or tights (waitresses). Feet are part of your 'working equipment'. Faulty socks (too tight, neglected holes, dirty) cause as much discomfort as unsatisfactory shoes.

Shoes These should fit well (with ample room for toe movement) and be a conventional style. Waitresses should avoid excessively high or pointed heels. (Stiletto heels damage floors and floor covering.) Have at least two pairs to allow for repair and for 'resting' a pair on alternate days. Keep in repair to avoid a 'down-at-heel' appearance and to ensure comfort and efficiency; and keep polished. Laced shoes give good support but waitresses may prefer black court (or similar plain style) shoes with medium heels.

Washable outer garments Frequently change and launder for immaculate appearance. Check that buttons are complete. Mend any tears or fraying where possible or replace.

Other garments If jacket, trousers or dresses cannot be laundered, regularly dry clean. Apart from stain removal this obviates stale smell or appearance. Pockets should be strong, desirably reinforced, to withstand use of order pads, bottle openers, cash. Outer garments should allow for free movement. Despite possible use of deodorants, waitresses should consider underarm shields for dresses. Underarm eyelets on synthetic fibre overalls or dresses allow air to circulate.

Pre-service care At each service, sponge and brush as necessary to remove spots. Check shoulders especially for dandruff or loose hairs. Make sure pockets are not bulging.

Jewellery

As with all who wear uniform (nurses, soldiers, etc.), waiting staff should not wear 'non-uniform' accessories. House rules vary but generally jewellery should not be worn by men or women except perhaps wrist watches of simple style, plain wedding rings (or signet rings) and plain 'keeper' earrings (if ears are pierced).

Hygiene

Hygiene involves care for the health of others and oneself. Waiting involves physical work, moving about, lifting trays. So look after your health; guard against leg or feet weaknesses; maintain good sight; and clean teeth and mouth. A balanced diet, fresh air, and suitable recreation all help.

Service must be done in a clean way to protect guests against food poisoning or passage of disease (Figure 10). Dirt and dirty practices make dining unpleasant as well as unsafe.

Management must conform with statutory requirements (i.e. the law, both national and local bylaws) covering premises, equipment, method and staff; however higher codes of clean practice than the law requires should be observed. Good staff support hygiene in all aspects of foods service.

Personal cleanliness and grooming when dealing with food is necessary at all times and in all catering establishments, not only at luxury level. Guests are not likely to return to a place where waiting staff are dirty.

Fingernails and hands

Fingernails and hands are always noticed by guests. Wash hands immediately before service and after using the toilet. Trim nails and cuticles neatly and keep clean with a nail brush. Waitresses should avoid nail varnish, clear or coloured, when on duty. Smokers must remove all traces of nicotine from fingers (pumice and bleach are useful).

Bodily cleanliness

Bodily cleanliness is essential. Any odour is an offence. A daily bath or shower should be the minimum. Talcum powder for body and feet is acceptable but avoid scent (even for a waitress).

Clear skin and complexion

A clear skin and complexion depends on good health based on adequate exercise, sleep, diet and cleanly habits. Use your leisure for fresh air recreation and feature fresh foods such as vegetables, fruit, wholemeal bread and milk in your diet. Waitresses should use cosmetics sparingly, only as consistent with a fresh appearance.

Hair

Hair should be neatly trimmed. Shampoo frequently (minimum weekly) to avoid dandruff and odour. Well brush as well as comb your hair. Avoid styles where hair falls over the eyes; tossing hair from the eyes, especially by hand, offends guests. Waitresses should adopt neat styles (free from adornment) in which hair does not fall on to or below the collar.

Mouth

Brush teeth at least twice a day certainly night and morning for a healthy appearance and wholesome breath. Inspection by a dentist is advisable twice a year and not less frequently than once a year. If worn, keep dentures scrupulously clean.

If you're handling food, stick to the rules!

1/ Always wash your hands before touching food, and always after using the WC.

2/ If you suffer from any skin, nose, throat or bowel trouble at work, tell your supervisor and *don't* handle food.

3/ Use waterproof dressings on cuts and sores. And remember to keep those dressings clean.

4/ Be clean in yourself *and* in the clothes you wear.

5/ Don't smoke in a kitchen or food room (in a catering establishment you'll be breaking the law !) ; and never cough or sneeze over food.

6/ Clean as you go in the kitchen ; if anything gets spilled, wipe it up immediately. See that all utensils are kept clean.

7/ Cover food, keep it clean, and serve it either cold or piping hot.

8/ Use tongs, spoons etc., when handling food, rather than your fingers.

9/ Always keep the lid on a dustbin.

10/ In catering establishments remember that clean, fully equipped, well-lit and airy conditions are required by law. But it's an environment that's right wherever food is being prepared.

Keep everything clean –
and you won't give germs a chance!

The Health Education Council
Helping you to better health
78 New Oxford Street, London WC1A 1AH

Figure 10 A Health Education poster, stressing the importance of hygiene.

Feet

Feet need care for comfort and cleanliness. Keep toe nails trim and feet well washed. Corns and other painful blemishes may require treatment by a chiropodist; for more serious foot weakness seek medical advice.

Pointers to personal practice

- Never lick fingers to separate checks, menus, etc.
- Keep hands *truly* clean (i.e. free from bacteria): never touch or pick at the face, facial spots, the nose
- Never fuss or touch the hair
- Protect cuts, boils, etc. on hands or body with clean, waterproof dressing
- Avoid using a handkerchief in a restaurant, but always carry a clean one (especially to smother an unavoidable cough or sneeze). Cold germs are quickly spread by 'spraying' through coughing or sneezing
- Do not drink, chew (or eat) on duty. Chewing is unsightly and suggests to guests that food is being touched and conveyed to mouths
- Never touch food, always use service equipment (e.g. spoon and fork)

Pests

Wage war against houseflies and vermin. Leave no food or food debris around to attract them. Report any signs of fly, vermin or insect infestation to management immediately.

Positive approach

'Dos and don'ts' cannot alone add up to clean restaurant practice. All concerned in food service should feel pride and responsibility in their job and be anxious to improve understanding of hygiene and health in promoting food sales and safety.

Personal factors

For your role as salesman and a welcoming approach to the guest, cultivate manners and appearance. A new personality is hard to acquire but you can develop agreeable facets of your own. This is particularly important for those aspiring to become a head waiter. Reading and interest in affairs of the day, sport and constructive recreations help. In your work:

- avoid airs and mannerisms
- be calm, polite and helpful to guests and fellow staff

- give additional attention when asked
- smile readily
- maintain high standards of grooming (see pp. 46–48 on hygiene and dress)
- stance, poise and deftness of movement are all important

Honesty

Observe strict honesty in billing and handling cash and in food and equipment. For example, do not take restaurant food for your own consumption in the establishment or at home; or 'borrow' silver or linen for similar purposes. This is stealing and denotes at the least that a waiter lacks a professional attitude.

Never be careless with the establishment's equipment because it is not your own.

Cooperation

Success depends on cooperation; so help your fellow workers.

- Do not be jealous if another waiter has customers who tip higher
- Take your turn in the kitchen servery queue for service
- Keep to the 'rules of the house' in spirit as well as in the letter
- If a mistake is made by your supervisor do not remonstrate with him in the restaurant. First, remedy the fault (e.g. bring the customer the dish that he states he ordered). Any explanation necessary to prevent an error recurring or to apportion blame should be made outside the restaurant, preferably after service.
- If you have any complaints to make to the head waiter or to colleagues, wait until service is over
- Study customers' preferences (even 'fads') – you will find they will be delighted when their wishes are anticipated

Conduct in the restaurant

Always be courteous to customers, but also carry good manners through to service room and locker room. Cultivate manners not only as a 'technique of the restaurant' but as second nature and to please those you contact.

- Treat every customer alike irrespective of his financial standing
- Never fawn on lavish tippers. Acknowledge tips graciously; if placed on the table do not remove until the customer has left
- Be forbearing with a critical or ill-tempered person
- Take pride in your work and do not treat it as an ordeal

Figure 11   The correct stance of a waiter.

Stance (Figure 11)

Good stance is important for appearance, comfort and efficiency. To stand upright and walk erect gives a good impression to guests and your bosses, and avoids the bodily stresses caused by slouching.

When not serving stand upright by your sideboard, with the service cloth folded on your left forearm, whether there are customers on your station or not.

- Never lean against walls or furniture
- Do not pass in front of a customer
- At all times give right of way to a guest
- When spoken to, stand erect and steady

Conversing

A courteous friendly approach to guests need not involve unnecessary chat. Avoid conversation with guests. Equally, do not converse, far less argue, with other staff.

- Never start a conversation with guests

- If a customer enters in conversation with you, answer politely but briefly. Tactfully excuse yourself at the first opportunity
- Never discuss other guests with customers, nor give information regarding guests
- Discipline yourself not to listen to guests' conversation, whether carried out loudly enough for you to hear or not
- Never use bad language either in the restaurant or in the dressing room

Speech and manners

Friendliness is paramount but must be compatible with courtesy. Exaggerated friendliness or familiarity is seldom appreciated. For example, waitresses, however 'popular priced' the establishment, should avoid using terms such as 'dear, dearie, ducks' to customers.

Waiting staff are constantly 'on show' but aim to be as unobtrusive as possible, quiet but clear in speech and restrained in manner.

- Never be servile, for as a good waiter, you should be proud of your skill; you are a technical salesman, and a good salesman aims to please
- Aim for a clear voice, low in pitch, with words precisely pronounced and ideas easily expressed
- Seek a sound knowledge of good English. Customers like to hear a well-modulated, pleasing voice, with well-expressed answers to any questions asked
- Knowledge of a second language is helpful, particularly where there are foreign visitors. (French is useful, for menus, dish repertoires and cookery books still have French terms)

Eating

Never eat on duty (this includes chewing gum).

Waiting attributes summarized

Waiters' knowledge should include:

- awareness of their sale's role, how to deal with guests
- product knowledge: foods, menus, cooking times and terms; wines and other beverages; cigars, tobacco
- product handling, that is methods of serving and clearing in restaurants, floors and lounges
- supporting routines, that is ménage (restaurant cleaning), mise en place

Waiters' qualities should embrace:

- warmth and courtesy
- appearance, cleanliness (grooming), deportment
- dexterity
- pride in the job
- honesty

Deportment and hygiene reminders

Although you should work unobtrusively, as a waiter you are under scrutiny by guests. Your dress and task make you more conspicuous than employees in other occupations. You 'perform' for an audience (often a critical one). In so doing, you represent your employer as well as yourself. Be proud of your work. Good service never requires a servile manner.

Clean practice helps to 'sell' you, your food and service. Observe the rules of hygiene already outlined especially when working before the public when your appearance (dress and cleanliness) should be beyond reproach.

Good humour shown by a friendly expression and a ready smile is part of the good waiter's stock-in-trade.

Conduct reminders

- Avoid a harried or harassed look
- Avoid mannerisms and eccentricities of dress, hair style and behaviour
- When not actually serving, stand upright by your station and never lean (especially not on sideboard, wall, table or back of chairs)
- Though keeping an eye on your tables to respond to guests seeking attention, avoid embarrassing guests by staring
- Never eat (nor chew gum, etc.) in the restaurant; smoking is strictly forbidden
- Avoid slovenly practices such as carrying spoons in pockets, menus in shirt fronts, pencil behind ears
- Walk with speed but without the impression of undue haste. Above all, *never* run; neither in the restaurant nor in the service area (a prime cause of accidents as well as creating a deplorable impression)
- Avoid unnecessary moving about (the less movement, the less fatigue); and keep to your own station as much as possible
- Cultivate quietness in manner, style of moving and in speech (modulated but clear)
- Avoid noise and unnecessary talk. Clattering cutlery, crockery, or trays signals ineptitude. Loud speech is equally offensive
- Do not initiate conversation with guests but respond courteously when addressed (without unduly prolonging conversation). Excuse yourself at the first opportunity

- Never discuss (nor give information about) other guests (or staff) with guests
- Never intrude into guests' conversation (show no sign of being aware of what guests may discuss together)
- Never chat with other waiters; confine talk with colleagues to the business in hand
- Avoid arguments with other waiters, that is never argue with nor complain to other staff, senior or junior, but make appropriate representations to the maître d'hôtel after service hours
- Raised voices, bad language, laughter (other than made discreetly to guests' remarks intentionally evoked) are taboo in the restaurant
- Treat all guests in the same fair and courteous way without favouring one against the other. Certainly do not show favour because of tips or anticipated tips.

Causes of offence

Bear in mind the positive qualities to cultivate as outlined previously; but check that you do not offend by lapses listed below. Waiting staff offend if they:

- forget to say 'thank you' or fail to acknowledge a tip
- cadge for tips, count tips or jingle coins in their pockets
- are bad tempered or indifferent
- talk too much to table guests when guests are talking to each other (i.e. are tactless)
- ignore guests by talking among themselves
- hurry customers to clear their 'stations' in order to leave early
- speak badly
- give bad service (i.e. on the wrong side of the diner), spill soup or other foods
- are dishonest, that is add up bills wrongly (against the customer)
- eat or chew during service
- put service cloths in trouser pockets or under the arm
- soil menus by careless use or keeping them in a pocket or their shirt fronts
- carry pencils behind their ears or in their hair
- neglect hygiene, that is have body odour; smelly feet; dirty or untidy hair; soiled hands and finger nails; have spotted clothes; fuss with hair or pick facial blemishes; sneeze or cough carelessly (do this into a handkerchief but otherwise avoid using handkerchiefs 'in the room' unless necessary); chew gum; or have dirty cuffs or shirt fronts (waiters), dirty aprons or hair bands (waitresses)
- are ill-clothed, that is have ill-polished shoes; wear high-heeled or otherwise unsuitable shoes; wear soiled or laddered stockings/tights;

wear jewellery (wedding rings and watches allowed)
- are bad timekeepers
- quarrel or are noisy on duty; shirk their allotted responsibilities.

See how many of these faults you notice when *you* are a customer. By avoiding faults, you not only please customers and employers, but pave the way to promotion.

7
Ménage and Mise en Place

Creating the right ambience for a restaurant through appropriate policies, design and décor needs the back-up maintenance, cleaning and preparation of the room before service. Management furnish and equip the 'room' and its ancillary departments, but waiting staff should appreciate what the tools of their trade are and how to maintain them and keep them clean.

Waiting service falls into three principal categories.

Pre-service preparation (mise en place)
Service to guests (the waiting operation)
Post-service clearance (including, possibly, a secondary mise en place for future meals)

This chapter deals with the first of these; but pre-service preparation may, itself, be divided into three subcategories.

Cleanliness and orderliness of the room
Checking and replenishing commodities (condiments, dressings, liqueurs, etc.) used during service
Pre-preparation of sideboards, tables, buffets, trolleys to be used during service

Tasks may be undertaken by single individuals for their station; or by groups for the benefit of the room as a whole (i.e. replenishment of condiment sets).

Preparatory duties

Apart from service at table, the waiter has other duties in preparing the restaurant, its furniture and equipment and which may include pantry and locker room. This is often called doing the ménage − literally the housework. In restaurants, as in kitchens, equipment or foods pre-prepared in readiness for service are described as mise en place (put in place). Hence, preparing is itself called in restaurant jargon 'doing the mise en place'. What has been so prepared is described also as mise en place or as being 'en place'.

Ménage tasks may be assigned to members of the restaurant brigade, particularly to junior staff; they are not carried out in waiting uniform but some protective dress, even if only an apron. Apart from assigned tasks (normally on a rota system), individual chefs de rang must ensure that their own section is properly cleaned, especially the sideboard and its contents.

Cleaning

At one time waiters had many responsibilities for cleaning, but these now vary according to whether an establishment is seasonal, high class or modest. Even when waiters do not have tasks concerned with cleaning and airing the restaurant, they should be aware of what is required and check that floors, walls, furniture, furnishing and equipment are clean and in good condition.

Evening routine

In restaurants where breakfast is not served or where a special breakfast room separate from the restaurant is available, the following routine should be carried out.

- Completely clear the restaurant tables the previous night
- Place salt cellars, peppers and other condiments on a table near the service doors, empty mustard dishes and wash (keep contents possibly in a jug)
- Remove flowers to the flower room (usually within the housekeeper's department)
- Place clean table cloths on top of one another on one table
- Place all the chairs on the tables, the seats resting on the table

Morning routine

On arrival in the morning, open all the windows to air the room, clearing cigar and other smells. Then each member of staff attends to his particular duty as detailed by the head waiter. These include:

Sweeping carpet or floor (if not done by domestic staff)
Dusting furniture, polishing mirrors and glass shelves, silver and glass show pieces, etc.
Cleaning and re-filling salts, peppers
Wiping necks and corks of sauce bottles
Making up fresh mustard and re-filling the pots
Cleaning certain articles of silver (in some operations all silver is cleaned by dining room staff)
Changing linen, re-stocking sideboards and dummy waiters
Preparing the cold buffet service
Sharpening knives (never done during service)
Setting the tables for lunch

When all the preparations are over (usually about 1 hour before the next service begins), close the windows and allow the room to reach comfortable warmth. Dining room temperature is around 18°C (65°F), possibly higher where American guests predominate.

Waiters then go to their dressing room to wash, tidy and clean their uniform. They should return to the dining room half an hour before service to:

- put finishing touches to stations
- attend to trolleys for sweet and plat du jour
- place cold dishes on the buffet

Lunch is usually served between 12 o'clock and 2.30 pm, in some cases even later.

Organizing mise en place

A head waiter usually organizes mise en place and ménage and assigns waiters to duties for a period (say a week at a time) on rota. One may be to look after cruets, another glass, another table linen, etc., subject to 'house' custom. A numbered list of tasks allocating them over precise periods (daily, weekly or monthly) simplifies drawing up duty rosters for commis and junior waiters, as shown by the samples in Figures 12 and 13.

In some restaurants, the station waiter is responsible for all duties for his section. A relief waiter takes charge of each section in turn when the station waiter has his 'day off'.

As a waiter, observe the following.

- Ensure that all equipment used on your tables is spotless
- Do not blame anyone else for dirty silverware, plates or glasses
- Rectify possible dullness yourself, but return anything not washed properly for re-washing

Allocating duties

TASK NUMBERS			
1	Dusting	9	Silver cleaning
2	Dusting	10	Silver cleaning
3	Sweeping	11	Silver cleaning
4	Cruets	12	Laundry
5	Cruets	13	Class
6	Plates for hot plates	14	Flowers
7	Plates for room	15	Etc. (other duties may be added or substituted to suit a particular organization)
8	Silver for kitchen		

Figure 12 Task numbers.

MÉNAGE DUTY ROSTER

Waiter's name	Mon.	Tues.	Weds.	Thurs.	Fri.
A. Brown	1	15	14	13	12
B. White	2	1	15	14	13
C. Gray	3	2	1	15	14
D. Black	4	3	2	1	15
E. Green	5	4	3	2	1
F. Smith	6	5	4	3	2
G. Jones	7	6	5	4	3
H. James	8	7	6	5	4
I. Potts	9	8	7	6	5
J. Baxter	10	9	8	7	6
K. Williams	11	10	9	8	7
L. Evans	12	11	10	9	8
M. Dick	13	12	11	10	9
N. Paul	14	13	12	11	10
O. George	15	14	13	12	11

Day of the week with task number

Figure 13 Ménage duty roster.

Figure 13 can be adapted for a six- or seven-day working week, or extended for larger brigades.

Duties must all finish together. Thus more people are allocated to duties taking more time, that is three on silver cleaning as opposed to one on glassware; or shorter tasks are grouped together.

Sweeping and dusting

Scrubbing floors and cleaning windows and walls are not waiters' normal duties; this is left to special cleaners. However, a waiter may sweep or vacuum the floor. If it is uncovered (e.g. parquet), a soft hair broom or dry mop and careful sweeping with the minimum of dust raising suffices. Use an electric polisher occasionally as directed.

To prepare for sweeping:

- remove any cloths, silver, etc. remaining on tables to the pantry
- place the chairs on top of the tables
- if labour and time permit, move the tables to one end of the room, place the chairs on top and sweep the clear half of the room
- move the chairs and tables to the clean half of the room and sweep the other half
- sweep rooms from the windows towards the service doors; push the broom and do not sweep the dust towards yourself

- dust will eventually pile up near the service doors, sweep it into a dust-pan
- when finished, replaced tables and chairs and dust them

When sweeping a carpet with a heavy broom, dust afterwards, for brooms throw up dust which collects on walls and curtains.

To prepare for vacuuming carpets:

- remove all match ends, pins, etc. from the carpet to avoid damaging the mechanism of the vacuum cleaner
- dust walls and curtains before the vacuum cleaner is used so that dust may descend to the carpet to be collected

Chairs

Dust not only the seat but under the struts of chairs so that no crumbs or dust are left. Wipe polished chairs with vinegar and water occasionally.

Restaurant furniture and equipment

What a restaurant contains is determined by factors such as price level, speed of turnover and style of service, among many others. Many up-market rooms will have a reception desk and a buffet; the first at, the second near, the entrance.

Reception desk

The high desk used by a reception head waiter is normally at the entrance. On it lies the table reservations book and a telephone. Keys for linen cupboard, condiment lockers, etc. are customarily kept in the desk drawer.

Buffet

A cold buffet table is also usually near the entrance where incoming guests can see at a glance what cold dishes are available. This long table is covered with a large tablecloth draped right down to the ground and is arranged just before lunch service.

It must be attractive. Use the most decorative dish as a centre-piece, flanked with other dishes on either side, and avoid overloading. You can create a raised centre by tiered shelves or boxes covered with white cloth.

Tables

Tables and sideboards are the waiter's work points. Table tops may be wood (usually covered with baize), or covered with glass or plastic.

Round tables are favoured in higher class establishments. Normally their sizes are:

710 mm (28 inches) to 760 mm (30 inches) diameter tables for one customer

900 mm (36 inches) to 1 m (40 inches) tables for two or three customers

1.10 m (44 inches) to 1.25 m (48 inches) tables for four or five, customers

up to 1.50 m (60 inches) for tables of six or seven customers (usually expandable to become oval for parties up to 14 or 15 guests)

In better class restaurants, each party has its own table and two parties are never made to share.

Popular restaurants may choose square or rectangular tables of uniform size; but these are not considered so intimate as round tables. Customers may sometimes be requested to share one table which can accommodate four guests. Two or more square tables can be put together quickly during service to accommodate large parties who have not reserved in advance.

Table sizes should allow:

- 534 mm ($1\frac{3}{4}$ ft) at least and desirably 610 mm (2 ft) length per cover for simple, plated service
- up to 760 mm ($2\frac{1}{2}$ ft) per person for silver service

Wider spacing tends to make guests feel isolated.

Cleaning tables

On glass-topped tables use a damp cloth followed by a polish with a dry cloth. Vinegar and water or ammonia and water may be necessary to remove stains, followed by a dry cloth polish. Wooden-topped tables require warm water, followed by a wax polish. Formica and similar stain-proof surfaces usually need only a damp cloth.

Sideboards (or dummy waiter)

Each waiter needs his own sideboard or station service table. He effects his preparations during service on an upper shelf, where a good space is necessary. An electric or spirit hot plate may be on this top surface.

Underneath are drawers or compartments, open or partially open at the front with the available table silver (cutlery) arranged inside.

Below the cutlery compartments is usually another shelf for plates, consommé and coffee saucers and so on.

Finally, on a bottom shelf, spare linen, tablecloths, napperons, service cloths, napkins, etc. are kept. In the back or side of a station sideboard may be a cupboard with a slot or flap for temporary storage of used linen.

Sideboard shelves are usually covered with white cloths made from old tablecloths. Napkins or tablecloths should not be used to cover the service table.

Clean side tables (accommodating table silver, linen, etc. for use during service) in the same way as other tables.

Mirrors, glass cases, etc.

Clean with a patent mirror glass cleaner or vinegar and water. Polish with a dry polishing cloth.

Flowers

Replenish water regularly. Keep vases clean. Take them out of the restaurant at the end of the day's service.

Their arrangement contributes to ambience and demands artistry that repays study. Some establishments employ a florist.

Linen changing

Linen is changed once, twice or three times daily according to the restaurant's size and quantity of stock. Count dirty linen carefully as it is changed on the basis of one clean for one dirty item. Usually a chef de rang and commis are appointed on a roster basis to look after dining room linen stock and for its change.

The linen changing duty follows the sequence given below.

- Collect, classify and count soiled table napkins, tablecloths and slips daily; usually recorded in a duplicate linen book
- Bundle into 'tens', after being scrutinized for tears or burns
- Take to the linen room where they are checked by the linen maid in the waiter's presence
- The amounts entered in the book being correct, the linen maid issues the same number of clean articles
- Once all linen has been changed the waiter's linen book is initialled and the top copy retained by the linen room, the duplicate remaining in the book
- Any discrepancy must be recorded so that missing linen can be obtained later

Pantry men change linen in the same way. In large establishments, waiters change their own waiter's cloths and aprons at the linen room. The linen room maid again gives clean for soiled.

Linen handling

Handle clean linen carefully for it is easily creased or soiled.

- Learn which size cloths belong to which tables
- Use napkins only for their correct purpose, i.e. for the customer, and sometimes for clean service such as on a plate carrying cutlery to and from the table
- Never re-fold used napkins and other used linen (slightly soiled napkins may get mixed with clean ones and given to a customer by mistake)
- Where a quantity of linen is held in reserve take care that it is used in rotation. Place fresh stocks under those already in the cupboard
- On no account use napkins as drying cloths. Various cloths are used for specific work: kitchen cloths for drying and polishing wet work; dusters (yellow) for dusting and dry polishing; linen (glass cloth) for glassware (cotton cloths leave fluff on the glass); and a waiter's cloth for use during service (see Chapter 12)

Cleaning check list

Check lists are drawn up to suit a particular establishment, but include such items as:

> floors: carpets or other surfaces are clean and free of marks
> dusting: chairs, table legs, sideboards, window ledges and other surfaces are clean
> polishing: mirrors, glass shelves, lamps and all metal, wood and plastic surfaces are polished
> airing: the room is aired (windows and/or doors)
> windows: cleanliness and working order
> table lamps and other lighting fittings: cleanliness and serviceability
> cutlery: polished for service
> réchauds and other service equipment: cleanliness and serviceability
> sideboards: cleanliness and order; necks, caps and stoppers clean

Checking that the above have been attended to is not only a matter for the supervisor but for all conscientious waiters.

8
Commodities and Equipment

Pre-service preparation applies also to a restaurant's contents; furniture, furnishings, silver, crockery, napery, glass and a small stock of consumable goods.

Condiments store cupboard

A restaurant holds a range of seasonings, sauces and even some sweet items; its ménage store or cupboard usually includes:

salt: both fine table salt and coarse rock salt (gros sel)
peppercorns, white and black
peppers: ground white, black and cayenne
English mustard
French mustards, strong (forte) and mild (douce)
vinegar, red and white wine vinegars
salad oil (olive, but possibly also ground nut oil (huile d'arachide) or corn oil)
sugar, caster and wrapped lump, speciality café sugars (including brown sugar)
proprietory sauces and relishes, i.e. Worcestershire sauce, tomato ketchup, Tobasco and other bottled sauces
chutneys, pickles, red currant jelly and mint jelly
herbs, spices and seasonings as required for any guéridon specialities

Perishable items

Indent daily or per meal according to menu requirements: butter for lamp cookery; oranges, lemons for speciality dishes; chopped parsley, grated cheese and other perishables.

Care of condiments

Keep cruets, bowls, bottles or other containers or holders of condiments and table commodities scrupulously clean, observing the following rules.

- Re-fill and wipe salt and pepper containers daily and empty and wash weekly. Completely empty and change, however, whenever the contents become lumpy or damp
- Check carefully the metal caps of glass salt cellars for signs of verdigris
- Wipe glass cruets daily and once weekly wash with vinegar solution and small lead shot, rinse well and drain, then place them sideways in or on a hotplate to evaporate all moisture before filling
- Empty, wash and then replenish English mustard for each meal service
- Between meal periods, wipe other containers, for example proprietory brand bottles and French mustard pots. Clean necks and mouths of chutney jars, bottled sauces and similar items. After the day's service, remove plated containers of preserves and sauces and their spoons for cleaning
- Re-fill and wipe sugar bowls daily and empty and wash weekly
- For weekly cleaning of silver or plated containers, dry-clean the empty cruets with plate powder taking care to brush the screw joint well; re-fill and replace top.

Silverware

'Silver' (often, in fact, stainless steel) is usually in AI silver-plating or hotel plate. Silver plating is thin but durable and with normal care lasts many years.

Table silver

Soup spoons: for soup when served in plates

Fish knives and forks: for fish and hors d'oeuvre

Large knives and forks: for entrées and main course (meat, poultry, etc.). Forks only for macaroni, gnocchi, etc. Fork with dessert spoon (or table spoon) for spaghetti

Dessert or sweet spoons and forks: for all sweets served on plates and oeuf sur le plat. Spoons alone for soup served in cups, hot and cold cereals

Small silver fruit knives and forks: for fresh fruit

Small knives for side plates for cheese and for savoury (used with a sweet fork)

Teaspoons: for teas, fruit cocktails, ice cream served as 'coupes', grapefruit, oeuf en cocotte, etc.

Sundae spoons: may be provided for ice cream desserts

Coffee spoons: for coffee

Service spoons and forks: for serving all food orders from the serving
dish onto the plate

Silver for serving food

Soup tureens, double and large
Individual soup bowls
Sauce boats and trays
Oval flats and covers
Oval or round vegetable dishes and covers
Soufflé cases, double
Oval or round under dish for vegetables
Oval or round entrée dishes
Oval or round under dishes for entrée
Round flats and covers

Silver for serving drinks

Salver for serving 25 cm (10 inches) diameter (round)
Salver for clearing 30 cm (12 inches) diameter (round)
Ice tongs for all ice drinks
Ice bucket and ice bucket stand

Still room silver

Coffee pots — 3 dl and 6 dl ($\frac{1}{2}$ and 1 pint)
Hot milk jugs — 3 dl and 6 dl ($\frac{1}{2}$ and 1 pint)
Tea pots — 3 dl, 6 dl and 9 dl ($\frac{1}{2}$, 1 and $1\frac{1}{2}$ pints)
Hot water jugs — 3 dl, 6 dl and 9 dl ($\frac{1}{2}$, 1 and $1\frac{1}{2}$ pints)
Cold milk jugs — 3 dl and 6 dl ($\frac{1}{2}$ and 1 pint)
Cream jugs — $\frac{1}{2}$ dl, $1\frac{1}{4}$ dl and 3 dl ($\frac{1}{12}$, $\frac{1}{4}$ pint and $\frac{1}{2}$ pint)
Toast racks — 5 bars, 7 bars and 9 bars
Egg cups

Special table silver

Sugar tongs for loaf sugar
Asparagus tongs
Grape scissors
Nut crackers
Pastry forks
Oyster forks
Finger bowls (can be glass)
Sugar bowls
Lobster picks

Lobster crackers
Set of cruets
French mustard spoons (but preferably bone)
Ice cream coupes
Pepper mills (can be of wood)
Sauce ladles $-\frac{3}{4}$ dl ($\frac{1}{8}$ pint)
Soup ladles
Gâteau slice
Pickle forks
Oil and vinegar sets

Miscellaneous equipment

Warm plate for service table
Methylated spirit lamp for preparation of dishes in front of customer
Chafing dish
Silver duck press
Silver hot trolley

Care of silver

Cut nothing on a silver dish as the slightest cut will injure the silver. Silver-plate is easily kept bright. Plate-room staff attend to large silver dishes, covers, etc., but cutlery and other special silver may be the responsibility of waiting staff.

Cleaning and polishing silver and cutlery

Many branded silver cleaners are used in private houses rather than by caterers. Cost is relevant when selecting a method. Some different methods are given below.

Burnishing machine

A revolving drum half filled with ball bearings for cutlery and small silver. It is rubber-lined so that the silver is not damaged during cleaning. A powder is used with hot water as the cleansing agent.

Polivit plate

A sheet of aluminium for large pieces of silver, such as flats, vegetable dishes and entrée dishes. It must be submerged in boiling water containing a strong solution of washing soda. The action of aluminium and soda quickly removes stains from silver. Any silver treated must be well washed afterwards.

Plate powder

Plate powder is used for large silverware or articles that cannot be cleaned by either of the first two methods, such as the silver parts of trolleys, methylated spirit lamps, cruets, bread boats (or silver baskets). It keeps a hard, bright shine on silver-plate, but takes too long for cutlery.

Method Free articles from grease. Rub briskly with a little moist plate powder (basically jeweller's rouge and whitening). When dry, remove all plate powder with a silver brush, especially from engravings, embossments, filigree, etc. Finally, polish hard with a soft cloth or, preferably, a chamois leather. Check that the brush has done its work; if greasy black marks arrive during brushing either the article was greasy (remove this with a warm moist cloth and re-brush the article) or the brush is dirty.

Care of cutlery

Dirty table cutlery is washed by plate-room staff; but not always satisfactorily for immediate re-use. To remedy, re-dip the silver in very hot water and polish briskly whilst hot and moist. This gives a hard shine and ensures thorough cleanliness.

Cutlery tarnishes through contact with eggs, sharp sauces, curries or from non-usage. Remove by the Polivit (aluminium sheet) technique in boiling water as described above.

Never mix knives with the other cutlery. Either place them in the solution (e.g. Polivit) separately or polish the handles by the plate powder method.

Plates

The several types used in food service include:

Soup plate: usually 230 mm (9 inches) for all thick soups, pot au feu (unless a marmite is used), mussels and oysters, Irish stew, Lancashire hotpot

Entrée plates: normally of 216 mm ($8\frac{1}{2}$ inches) size for hors d'oeuvre, fish and entrées as subsidiary courses, as a soup under plate, as a cover plate and service plate

Meat or fish plate: usually 254 mm (10 inches) for main course service

Sweet plate: for sweets and puddings (often the 216 mm ($8\frac{1}{2}$ inch) plate is used)

Dessert or fruit plate: (often of different design, e.g. Bavarian fruit pattern)

Tea plate: 178 mm (7 inches) size for cheese, bread rolls

Salad plate: half-moon

Cups

The four kinds of cups for beverage service are:

> soup cup: (two handles), 3 dl ($\frac{1}{2}$ pint)
> breakfast cup: plain pattern, 3 dl ($\frac{1}{2}$ pint)
> tea cup: floral, dainty pattern, $1\frac{1}{2}$ or $1\frac{2}{5}$ dl ($\frac{1}{4}$ or $\frac{1}{3}$ pint)
> coffee cup: floral, dainty pattern, $\frac{3}{4}$ or $1\frac{1}{4}$ dl ($\frac{1}{8}$ or $\frac{1}{6}$ pint)

Care of crockery

Make certain that your china is spotless. If not dried thoroughly after washing, it becomes dull, spotted or streaky from residual washing powder. Rectify by wiping the china with a warm moist cloth and polishing. A dry cloth only, seldom removes the marks. If the china still has particles of food on it, send it back for re-washing. Carefully inspect cups to ensure that there is no lipstick left on. Do not use cracked or chipped chinaware.

Glassware

The reader is referred to Chapter 18 for further details of glass for liquor service.

Wash glasses in warm water (not too hot), rinse in clean hot water, and then dry with a linen cloth. A cotton cloth does not absorb enough water to polish properly and leaves fluff behind. Pantries may have a teak sink for glass as wood is softer than metal and helps prevent breakages; but the metal sink of softer type is now widely used.

Water jugs take a 'water line' of chalk or other hard substances in water; if the jug has a 'neck' (preventing the hand to enter easily), clean with potato peelings, finely cut, swilled round the jug with water.

Trays

Wine waiters use trays or salvers for the service of drinks served in glasses (whisky, gin, aperitifs, beer, minerals, etc.) and also for removing dirty glasses from tables. Wine waiters' trays are round, in effect salvers, usually from 30 cm (12 inches) to 46 cm (18 inches), the larger size normally being used for clearing.

Otherwise waiters use of trays is confined mostly to breakfast or afternoon tea service, when a rectangular type is used. These square or rectangular trays are sometimes used for carrying food from kitchen servery to sideboard during meal service and also for clearance of dirties from the restaurant.

Trays used for carrying food and dishes should be covered with a clean napkin.

Tray cleaning

Clean metal trays with metal polish; silver salvers with plate powder. Stainless alloy trays require only a wash and polish. Clean wooden trays with a damp cloth and polish with a dry cloth. Take care that aluminium alloy trays are never cleaned in the soda tank or they will blacken and be ruined.

Other equipment

(Equipment made in a variety of material, including silver)

Ash trays
Bread boats
Casseroles: for prepared food and sauces
Cheese scoops
Crumb scoops
Flower vases
Fruit stands
Ice coupes
Tea strainers
Wine cradles
Wine funnels

Stock-taking

Management require regular stock-taking in the restaurant for reference and replacements. Usually once a month, after the end of a day's service, equipment is laid out on tables in tens for counting, recording and checking against the inventory.

Service room or pantry

A service room or pantry contains:

- shelves or cupboards for stacking glassware, etc.
- a table (often of two tiers) to take dirty plates and silver brought in from the restaurant
- a box or boxes for dirty table silver
- bins for rubbish
- sinks with hot and cold water and draining racks for washing glasses

If a small service lift is used, shelves should be alongside to facilitate service during peak hours.

The glass pantry may be a separate unit staffed by those used to handling glassware.

A large linen box (similar to a post box but with a larger 'mouth') should stand in one corner to receive table napkins, tablecloths, etc. If it has a flat top, this box can be used for extra service space.

A 'hot plate' (a specially heated table-cupboard with a hot flat top, inside which a supply of hot plates can be kept) is essential.

Two doors should connect the service room with the restaurant: one for waiters going from the service room to the restaurant and the other for their return and marked with the words 'In', 'Out'. To use the wrong door can cause clashes and serious accidents. Figure 14 illustrates a well designed service room or pantry.

When you leave the restaurant with used materials, put dirty plates properly stacked on the table provided and dirty silver in the appropriate boxes. (To save fatigue and breakages these tables and boxes should be near the exit door from the restaurant and between the door and service lift.) Then go to the service table in the servery or kitchen to collect the next set of dishes ordered by the customer, take the plates from the hot plate and re-enter the restaurant.

Pantry maintenance

Shelves should be cleaned and articles kept there (e.g. cruets and condiments) put in order for quick service. Wash floor and shelves daily. Wash stainless steel or aluminium hot plate and clean with emery paper made of steel and clean the sinks. Wash tiled walls weekly.

Larger establishments often employ a pantryman or woman who, during rush hours, when waiters are busy, help to keep the pantry clear of dirty dishes and silver.

Dispense bar

A dispense bar or 'wine stores control' often adjoins the pantry so that waiters can collect orders for wines, beers, minerals, etc. as ordered by customers.

Maintenance checking

Apart from daily and pre-service checking, managements may call for the supervisor to complete check lists at longer intervals.

Weekly check

A weekly check might include:

Entrance: doors in good repair and clean

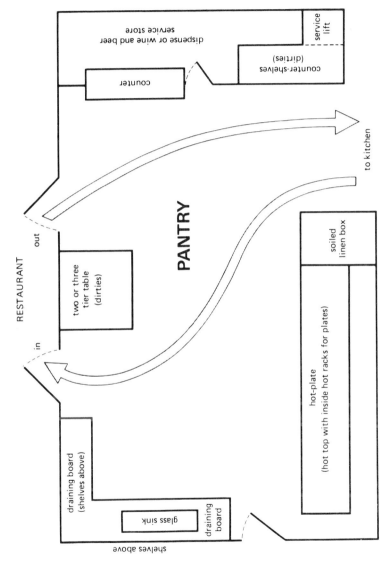

Figure 14 Plan of a service room or pantry.

floors (including steps if any) sound and covering (carpets, etc.) clean and in good repair

lighting adequate and in repair

reception desk or stand − check phone, reservation book and other records; cleanliness and tidiness

Restaurant: heating/air conditioning in good order (cleanliness of vents, etc.)

floors (including windows), ceilings and their surfaces in good decorative order and clean

lighting − bulbs replaced, cleanliness, repair

tables − tops (baize, etc.) in good repair, clean, legs sound and clean

sideboards − repair, cleanliness

chairs − sound repair, firm, upholstery clean

trolleys − carving wagons, etc., cleanliness, repair

furnishings (mirrors, pictures, etc.) − glazing uncracked, clean

silverware − plating sound, good repair, clean, adequate quantity

crockery − check quantity, check for cracking, discoloration, etc.

cutlery − as silverware

Pantry: appliances serviceable (lift, hot plate, burnishing machine, plate wash, etc.)

glassware − check quantity, for chips and cracks

sinks − unblocked, cleanliness

The adequacy and good order of the 'room', ancilliary departments and all equipment and stock is an essential basis for effective food and beverage service.

9
Lay - Up of Sideboard and Table

When the restaurant is clean, a waiter must then prepare for service. Some of the following instructions apply to more elaborate service, but many are appropriate to good waiting anywhere.

The sideboard
(or service station side table)

In small restaurants a service table, holding sauces, extra plates and other requirements, may be placed for the use of all waiters, but each station should have its own sideboard. A typical sideboard is illustrated in Figure 15.

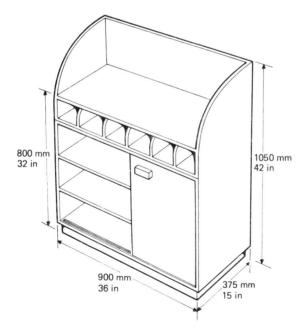

Figure 15 A typical sideboard.

Before any customers arrive, the sideboard should be 'en place', that is, all the equipment that may be required during service arranged 'in place' according to a plan or sequence. All sideboards should be uniform so that there is no confusion when waiters change stations or are relieved on days off.

Sideboard stock

Items commonly required on the sideboard include:

ashtrays
bread baskets
* bottle openers
butter dishes
* corkscrew
condiments: Worcestershire sauce, Tobasco sauce, tomato ketchup and other proprietory sauces, pickles, horseradish sauce, chutney, etc.
cruet: salt, pepper, oil, vinegar, mustard (French and English)
cutlery: soup, dessert, sundae and tea spoons; fish knives and forks; table knives and forks; side knives, coffee spoons; and special items as required, for example oyster forks, lobster picks
doyleys
fingerbowls
glassware: water jug
linen: napkins (serviettes), napperons, tablecloth
* matches
order (check) pad
* pencil
* service cloths
service equipment: tablespoons, forks
trays

Sideboard check

Before service ensure that your sideboard is fully stocked for service and carry out the following.

Check your supply of silver (particularly sufficient service spoons and forks), cold joint plates, fish plates, side plates, coffee saucers
Check that sugar bowls are filled
Ensure there is a supply of finger bowls (half slices of lemon ready for the edge of the bowl)
Switch on hotplates about 15 minutes before service

* Items asterisked are commonly carried by the waiter

Linen

Having obtained linen as described earlier (see p. 63):

(see p. 63)

check the number and sizes of the pieces given
ensure that they are all in serviceable condition
sort, according to sizes, and neatly stack on the side-table.

Silver

Obtain silver from the plate room (silver pantry), ensuring that every piece is clean. Sort knives, forks, spoons, etc. and place them in the respective compartments or drawers. How cutlery is placed varies according to sideboard compartments available, but should always conform to a pattern.

- Keep handles towards the outer part of the drawer, the prongs of forks and spoons facing sideways
- Items placed at the left of a cover when setting a table are similarly placed to the left in the sideboard
- Cutlery placed at the right of a cover are similarly placed to the right in the sideboard
- Observe this sequence in the same way in all the sideboards in the room

Avoid placing more than one item in one compartment, but if shortage of compartments makes this necessary, then observe logical pairing; for example, pair service spoons with service forks and fish knives with fish forks; do not pair items stocked in large numbers such as meat knives and forks.

Other items

Obtain ice bowls, rolls of bread, butter, water, doyleys, depending on the kind of establishment, and place in readiness on the side-table. Place ice in the water to keep it cool.

Table preparation

The table, which provides a frame for meals, is the focal point of both the guests' enjoyment and waiters' work. This important setting for sales must be well prepared to be both attractive and functional.

Table laying is usually a group exercise for a brigade of waiters. Each person will take an allotted task throughout the room.

Some restaurants use dining tables covered with a cloth, others use tables, generally polished, on which the plates are placed with or without an under-mat. For fine wood tables, underpads for heat insulation are desirable for protection and sound deadening.

Tables to be covered with a cloth should be fitted with baize or felt to:

- deaden noise of plates, cutlery and glass placed on them
- keep the cloth in position, to hang evenly without slipping
- cushion the guests' wrists from sharp edges of the table

Before covering and laying tables (with their chairs)

- ensure that they are correctly aligned for access
- obtain the cloths or mats (usually from the linen room)

Place mats

Laying place mats is not as formalized as for tablecloths:

- ensure that the table surface is clean and without streaks
- place the mats 1.25–2.5 cm ($\frac{1}{2}$ –1 inch) from the table's edge and parallel to it and squarely before each guest's chair, that is, exactly where the plate, bowl, glass, etc. are later to be set

Tablecloths

As a table creates a framework for what is to be served on it, plain white table-cloths have two prime qualities. They:

- provide an excellent background for glass, silver, china, flowers and, ultimately, wine and food
- readily reveal dirt. Spotless white napery emphasizes hygiene and a pleasant appearance

Coloured and patterned linen has its place in décor, but white or pastel shades are favoured for a background 'canvas' for the picture to be created in table lay-up.

Napperons

A table slip (napperon) saves laundry costs. Designed to be laid over the tablecloth, it is smaller than a normal square tablecloth by 90 cm (3 feet) (i.e. the length of the overhang of a cloth from its edge down the table legs). It is therefore found in various sizes. A common size is 91.5 cm (36 inches) by 91.5 cm (36 inches) and seldom is it larger than 122 cm square (48 inches square).

The napperon originally provided clean covering when coffee was served at a meal's close. Nowadays, after a table has been used, a clean napperon may be placed to cover the tablecloth; thus a tablecloth may remain on for a whole meal service or even throughout a day, unless spillage has badly soiled it.

Decorative effects may be achieved by using napperons (and table napkins) of colours to contrast or blend with tablecloths.

Disposables

For further laundry economy and to avoid problems of linen dispatch and delivery, disposable (paper) slip cloths and table napkins may be considered.

Preparing for cloth laying

Before laying a cloth make sure that the table is correctly placed in line with other tables and correctly angled and steady to avoid handling it once laid. (A small round of cork can steady the short leg of a table.)

Laying the cloth

To avoid creasing the cloth, which spoils the table's appearance, handle as little as possible when laying (Figure 16). To facilitate putting on the cloth, tablecloths are normally screen folded (W) with the face (polished) side outside. Ensure that the tablecloth is the right side up. The right side is more highly laundered and the hem is on the underside. The folds should be centred on the table with the points at the corners so that eventually the cloth will hang evenly over the table legs.

Your aim in laying is to cover the four table legs with the cloth's four corners hanging about 7.5–10 cm (3 or 4 inches) from the floor.

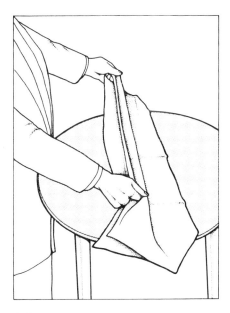

Figure 16   Laying a cloth.

Position and procedure

To place the cloth on the table, adopt the following procedure.

- Stand centrally *between* two legs
- Open out the cloth to its length across the table with the two double folds facing away
- On *your* side are the two woven edges with a double fold inside
- Take the top flap between thumbs and first fingers with the thumbs uppermost and the central folds between the first and second fingers
- Keeping your arms outspread the width of the table, lift the cloth and place the bottom flap (which is lying loose) over the far edge of the table
- Let the rest of the cloth lie on the table
- Release your hold on the centre folds and gently draw the top flap across the table until the whole cloth is opened out
- Inspect to see that the drop is even all round and that the table legs are covered
- Place the chairs in the correct positions

Changing the cloth during service (Figure 17)

When a soiled tablecloth has to be changed during service, adopt the following method.

- Clear any articles on the table to the sideboard (never place them on chairs or on the next table)
- Brush the cloth, if necessary, onto a crumb tray or plate

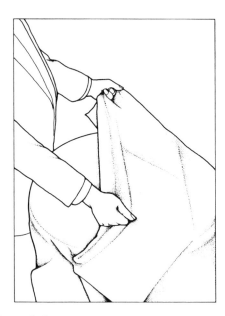

Figure 17   Changing a cloth.

- Open out the clean cloth (hold between the fingers as described above)
- Hold the loose underflap clear over the far edge of the table and release the centre folds
- Holding the edge of the cloth between thumb and fingers, the rest of the cloth will fall lightly onto the chair
- Then grip the soiled cloth at the far outer edges between the back fingers and the palm and draw both cloths across the table. (As the clean cloth reaches its position, the soiled cloth will drop from underneath)
- Inspect the clean cloth for correct drop

Types of cover

When all the cloths are laid, table mise en place begins. Tables are laid neatly and geometrically according to the requirements of the establishment. This is normally done *en masse* during the 'closed period'; and a waiter usually deals with only two items throughout the room.

Place settings are known as covers (in French, couverts), which define the space for each guest's table space and the crockery, silver, glass, cutlery and napkin layed for him.

The two principal types of cover for main meals are determined by whether the menu is à la carte or tâble d'hôte, that is whether a customer selects from a wide choice of individually priced items (à la carte) or pays a fixed price for a set meal of a number of courses (table d'hôte).

Cover space

Space on a table for an individual cover is variable. Domestic dining tables are normally made in multiples of 45.75 cm (18 inches), which is too narrow for professional service; 61 cm (24 inches) is the minimum practicable even for simple plate service.

On a round table, always place the covers between the legs which should provide not less than 61 cm (24 inches). On long rectangular tables allow 66 cm (26 inches) to 76.25 cm (30 inches) for each individual; 76.25 cm (30 inches) is the normal minimum for good class silver service.

The table is the first thing a customer sees when sitting down. First impressions can make or mar his opinions as to the service he can expect. A tidy table usually means a conscientious waiter; an untidy table, an untidy and careless waiter.

Plates for covers

When laying covers for a main meal, adopt the following procedure.

- Place an entrée-sized 'show plate' at each cover 1.25 cm ($\frac{1}{2}$ inch) from the edge of the table, exactly central before the guest's chair

- Place remaining items symmetrically around this guide plate
- Check and polish plates at the sideboard; never put cracked plates on the table
- If plates are badged, place badges uppermost facing the guest (12 o'clock position) when he is seated

Setting silver

Then lay the silver.

- Carry clean, polished cutlery in a clean service cloth in one hand (never in bare hands) (Figure 18)
- Handling only at the base, place cutlery at the correct position round the table (Figure 19)
- Always place salt and pepper cruets on the table; for a long table allow one set for each two covers. (If individual cruets, i.e. salt and pepper, are required, place them centrally just above the dessert fork and spoon)

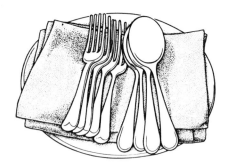

Figure 18   Plate prepared with service gear.

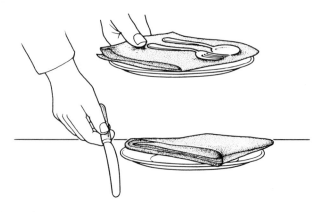

Figure 19   Laying a cover.

- Do not leave mustards or sauces, including those in bottles or jars, on tables; however, pass them at the time as the course may require, and remove immediately when this course is completed

Table d'hôte covers

A table d'hôte setting is intended to cover all the principal courses so lay the table in advance to cover all soup, fish, meat and sweet courses (Figure 20a). For a pre-arranged party, set up the complete cover except for the sweet fork and spoon. Observe the following.

- Cutlery on the outside must always be what is required for the next course
- If a 'show plate' is not used, the distance between the inside knife and fork should be 23 cm (a good 9 inches) and the sweet or dessert silver (spoon and fork) should also be 23 cm (9 inches) from the table's edge, that is, a plate space should be about 23 cm (9 inches) square.
- Do not spread tableware out but group cutlery closely
- Note the position of the second fork in Figure 20a.

Figure 20(a)   Table d'hôte cover.

Sequence of settings

- Begin with the joint knife on the right of the entrée or 'show plate' 1.25 cm ($\frac{1}{2}$ inch) from the edge of the table with the sharp edge of the blade turned towards the plate
- Place the fish knife next to the joint knife
- Place the soup spoon next to the fish knife
  (All these should be near one another without actually touching and all 1.25 cm ($\frac{1}{2}$ inch) from the edge of the table)
- To the left of the 'show plate' or the left of the cover, place the joint fork 1.25 cm ($\frac{1}{2}$ inch) from the edge of the table

- Place the fish fork next to the joint fork (up a little so that the top of the prongs is in line with the tip of the joint knife)
- Place the sweet fork in front of the plate with the handle towards the left of the cover
- Align the dessert spoon above it but with handle towards the right
- Place the side plate to the left of the cover
- Place the side knife on the plate
- Position the water goblet or wine glass, turned upside down, just above the tip of the joint knife at the top right-hand side. (Some establishments may require both a water (say 2.25 dl) and a wine goblet (say 1.5 dl), in which case place the smaller immediately to the right and a little further from the knife tips than the larger glass)
- Place a folded napkin on the 'show plate'
- Finally, place a cruet set (salt and pepper only) and an ash tray in the centre of the table

In the morning about half an hour before lunch, the vases of flowers are collected from the flower room and placed around the room.

American settings

Lay-ups are basically the same everywhere but there are subtle differences in various restaurants, so a waiter must be able to adapt himself to the methods employed.

In American table settings, for example, a coffee cup and saucer (not demi-tasse size) may also be placed centrally to the right of the soup spoon.

À la carte covers

In à la carte service a minimum of silver is put on the table beforehand, an hors d'oeuvre cover or a fish knife and fork suffices (Figure 20b). Place the necessary cutlery in position after you know the customer's requirements. Do not lay them all in advance, but only as required for each course and at the time of service.

Figure 20(b)   A la carte cover.

Other cutlery, when put on course by course as the meal progresses, is brought to the table by the waiter on a napkin-covered service plate. This napkin-covered plate is used for every article placed on or removed from the table.

This kind of 'à la carte' lay-up procedure is also used in fashionable restaurants whether they are dealing with the tâble d'hôte menu or an à la carte menu or both.

Other than the covers, the rest of the à la carte table lay-up is the same as for table d'hôte service. However, some restaurants featuring specialities may require additional cutlery for, say, a seafood item.

Completing the table

Laying up creates a picture. Everything on the table should be sparkingly clean and arranged symmetrically, that is, tableware laid in vertical and horizontal lines and items ancillary to the covers (cruet, flowers, etc.) placed to balance (Figure 21).

Positioning the general items depends on table size and the number of covers. Aim for a symmetrical design, convenient and pleasing to guests.

For tables of twos and fours, place the cruet (salt and pepper only), ashtray and flowers centrally. For a table of three, arrange these to balance any 'blank' sides, but in a readily accessible position for guests, that is, with the flower vase furthest away.

Figure 21 Table lay-up. Lay on the outside the cutlery used first: soup spoon, fish knife and fork, meat knife and fork. Dessert spoon with handle to right, that of fork to left; small knife on side plate.

Since the table's appearance helps to create mood and 'sells' the restaurant and its fare, promotional or other items can be added such as:

- electric table lamps or candles (in unusual candlesticks or glass 'vigil' holders)
- 'house' matches placed near covers
- table 'tents' (folders of card or paper) advertising a restaurant's or hotel's specialities; wine by the glass (or quarter bottles); or forthcoming attractions or function facilities

Relaying covers during service

Changing a tablecloth during service has already been described. Such a change involves re-laying the covers; but even without a cloth change or if only a napperon is used to cover a soiling mark, settings need to be re-laid.

Remember during service never to carry cutlery in your hand nor even in a cloth; always carry cutlery on a salver or large plate covered with a serviette to deaden any noise.

Arrange the re-lay silver neatly on the salver with the spoons and forks in line on their sides and knives and fish knives tucked underneath at right angles on either side. This facilitates handling, allays noise, possible accident and also looks neater.

- First replace the flowers, cruet, etc.
- Then relay cutlery, one couvert at a time from the cloth-covered salver.

Napkin folding

Napkin folding is today criticized because of:

- hygiene − excessive handling by waiters
- cost − unproductive use of restaurant staff time and labour

Nevertheless, there remains a demand for, and consequently use of, decorative folds for napkins on place settings, especially at functions. Otherwise a simple single roll, as portrayed in the table settings, remains a most effective way of placing and presenting a napkin.

A table napkin for folding must be no less than 66 cm × 66 cm (26 × 26 inches) square. An example of a simple treatment is the lunch fold.

Lunch fold (Figure 22)

- Fold the napkin into three, keeping the crease at the top (otherwise the finish is untidy)
- From the middle of the top edge, fold one side down
- Repeat from the other side so that the ends are level

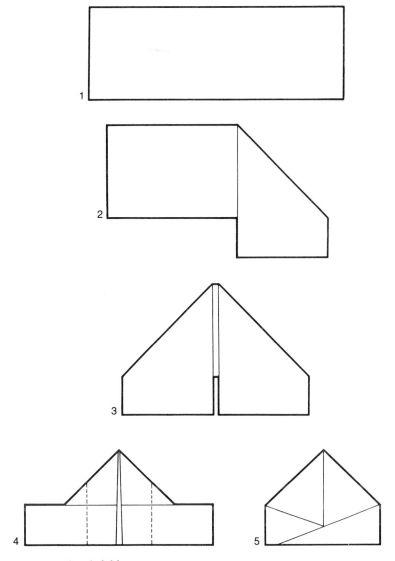

Figure 22   The lunch fold.

- Fold these ends in two to be level with the bottom of the original fold
- Next, fold in three as indicated by the dotted lines in Figure 22 so that one end rests on the end of the other
- Tuck one side into the other so that each end stops the other from opening

Flowers for the table

Flowers and their containers can be 'overdone'. Bowls and arrangements on restaurant tables should be low so as not to restrict guests' view of each other; Neither must flowers crowd the table. They must leave space for necessities such as cruets.

Single roses floated in water in a brandy balloon, a small trail of flowers laid on the table surface itself, or flowers in small 'unusual' containers are all possibilities. In the continental tradition, head waiters themselves bought and arranged fresh fruit and also took pride in arranging flowers (and petal 'pictures' on table surfaces). Some restaurateurs maintain this tradition; others rely on staff florists or floral contractors.

The following procedures should be adopted.

- Cut stems of flowers on the slant with a sharp knife
- Remove leaves that would otherwise be below water level
- Keep flower vases and water clean
- Place flowers to be stored overnight in warm water 45°C (110°F) and allow to stand in a cool place

For the table, avoid flowers which are too large, tall or heavily perfumed.

Final routine and check

Shortly before guests are due to arrive:

- turn up glasses left upside down during mise en place and give them a final polish
- place toast Melba and butter on the tables before the beginning of the meal, but never before the customer has occupied his table, whether reserved or not
- if bread or rolls have not been placed on side plates as part of the cover, pass them at the beginning of the meal and during the meal as required

Check the laid table:

- everything on it should be scrupulously clean and well arranged
- covers should face one another across the table when four places are set
- if there are only two covers, they should face the centre of the room and not a wall or door
- flowers, cruets and other items should be placed to balance the setting

Personal check

Ensure that you are personally 'en place' in hygiene, dress and equipment – that is, you carry on yourself matches (or a lighter), a pencil (or ballpoint pen), a bottle opener/corkscrew, a clean service cloth.

Brief yourself thoroughly on the day's menu, the meaning of all dish designations and what constitutes the garnishes. Thus, be aware of what you have to sell. This is what the dining room, its stations and table preparations support.

10
Receiving Guests and Taking Orders

Once the restaurant is *en place* and open, the waiting staff are ready to serve customers. The prime task is to make customers welcome.

Reservations

In large, first class establishments, one or more head waiter may be engaged in receiving guests. This reception head waiter takes and enters advance bookings in a reservation book.

Policy for telephoned or other advance table reservations should be consistent with a clear time limit for holding tables. For first sittings at opening hours, tables are not held for longer than 15–30 minutes, unless business is slack.

It is not usual to accept reservations once service for luncheon or dinner has started; though some restaurants may make reservations for second or even third seatings when evening service extends over a long period and dining patterns are known.

Respond courteously to telephone enquirers after normal booking time, saying that you will try to provide a table when the party arrives; adding a sentence such as 'I look forward to greeting you here later this evening (or afternoon), Sir'.

In dealing with telephone calls requesting reservations or information, your response should be warm and interested. Note the guest's name and insert it on the table reservation list or plan.

Similarly, make welcome a late arrival, even one who appears just before service hours end, give him proper service and do not make him feel hurried.

Choice of table

Actual placing depends on vacancies at the time, the size of the party and, as far as possible, the wishes of the guests. Some may prefer quiet corners, others to be near an orchestra or by a window.

- Ascertain or gauge the wishes of guests
- Use your discretion so that well-mannered/pleasing guests are more conspicuously placed than those less so. ('Sizing up' guests and their wishes is acquired by experience)
- Do not place at different tables a group of guests who wish to sit together
- When the restaurant is busy you should know when suitable places will become vacant or be ready to extend and prepare a table to accommodate a larger number

Greeting

Greeting is often a duty of the maître d'hôtel or a reception head waiter; but restaurant receptionists, seaters or 'greeters' may be employed. Any waiter, however, should be familiar with 'greeting and seating'; someone should always be positioned at the restaurant entrance to receive arrivals.

Guests may be shy on entering a busy restaurant under the gaze of others, particularly for the first time; so aim to make them welcome and at ease.

Observe the following points.

- Welcome with 'good afternoon (or good evening as appropriate) Mr/Mrs Brown', that is by name if known (or Sir or Madam if not known)
- Enquire if a reservation has been made and for how many by adding 'How many in your party, please?' Vary the greeting to suit the occasion
- To a single arrival, avoid saying 'Just one?' or 'Are you alone?' to avoid emphasizing 'aloneness'
- To young children, simply 'Good morning' (or other time of day)
- Greet in a smiling, friendly (not exaggeratedly effusive) manner
- Do not allow tipping to influence seating priority which should accord with reservation sequence or, when no reservation, sequence of arrival
- Never ask guests to wait when there are unreserved and empty tables available
- If the restaurant is full and no reservation has been made, advise guests of the likely waiting time. Suggest that they may care to wait in the bar or lounge
- When guests wait in the bar, you may present the menu, allow time to study it and take the meal order in the bar itself. This is convenient for guests, reduces delay at table and aids table turnover

Seating

As a greeter, your actions should be as follows.

- When and if there is a vacant table properly laid, lead the party to it; but do not seat them at any table showing signs of previous use

- On arrival at the table, draw out chairs (for ladies first)
- Move the chairs forward as guests seat themselves, again first for ladies
- Help any lady who may wish to remove her coat
- If you are not to take the order, summon the wine waiter, station head waiter or waiter; however, you will normally ask 'May the wine waiter serve you with an aperitif, sir?'

Seating parties with children

Fashionable restaurants may wish to seat parties with children inconspicuously; otherwise parental patronage may be secured through children being welcomed and looked after. Children grow up to become patrons themselves. A family trade needs facilities like high chairs for seating smaller children.

Reception at table

Once the greeter has 'handed over' the party to the station head waiter or station waiter, the guests are again greeted, always courteously, never with ill humour or signs of boredom. Guests are gratified to be recognized and named. So greet as indicated on p. 91 under greeting.

Possible problems

To avoid problems of dissatisfied customers, the following points should be noted.

- Never ignore arrivals nor give the impression that they are being overlooked
- If service pressure at other tables prevents your attending to guests immediately, assure them that you will do so as soon as possible
- When two tables are occupied at approximately the same time, take the order of the first party first. Customers are irritated by failure to observe a 'first come, first served'
- Work as a team member and assist others whenever possible to keep a constant contact with all clientele

Customers are annoyed if a waiter passes without showing awareness that they are not receiving attention; as may happen when a busy waiter from a different station is passing an occupied table not on his station. In such a case, stop, acknowledge the call and say politely 'I will send your station waiter to you, sir'.

Cooperation between staff is essential to smooth service, but to avoid confusion waiters should not 'overlap' other stations.

Types of food orders

Before considering your next actions as a waiter in preparing to take, prepare for and serve the guest's food order, you should know about the menu and what is on it and be able to advise guests. Broadly, food orders fall under one of the following categories.

À la carte   When a customer orders à la carte he chooses the dishes he desires from all those on the menu. His charge for the meal will be the total of the prices of dishes served to him.

Table d'hôte   In table d'hôte service, the customer chooses from a more restricted list (usually divided into courses) and pays a fixed, inclusive charge.

Plat du jour   On the à la carte menu there may be a dish of the day (plat du jour). This can also be a main dish of the table d'hôte meal. When the plat du jour is on the à la carte menu at a fixed price, it is often less than the price normally charged on other days. Potatoes and vegetables as a garnish are often included in the price. This dish is always a 'ready dish'. It is not a means of getting rid of 'left overs'.

Orders and selling

Thus, you must be familiar with the menu; its range and prices, composition, method of preparing and cooking dishes. You may need to enquire about such dishes as steaks and chops 'How do you like them cooked, sir – under, medium or well done?' You can then advise guests if they need any help. You should always have the appropriate accompaniments to hand on your service station. You may also help sell food and service by:

- knowing seasonable dishes
- suggesting dishes suitable for particular requirements, for example, those ready for quick service to those in a hurry or items suitable for children
- giving salads, vegetable and potato suggestions for grills, roasts and main courses for à la carte guests
- knowing selections for the dessert course when this stage is reached by à la carte customers

Awaiting the order

After the aperitif enquiry, place menus (ensuring they are clean) from the left. When menus are lengthy, allow customers a few minutes before asking for the order. In good class establishments, when guests have just been

received and are considering their requirements, as the waiter and according
to 'house' custom, you will:

- *from the left*, place fresh butter on the table
- pass bread rolls or place toast Melba on the table
- assist by unfolding table napkins, offering or helping to place them for
  guests
- *from the right*, fill water glasses

In more modest establishments and where, for example, butter is not
included but is a charged item, then this procedure may be modified.

Check that the table is fully and correctly laid.

How to take the order

When guests lay the menu flat on the table, it usually signifies that they are
ready to order. When it is apparent that there is a host, take his instructions
first, otherwise receive orders as guests as ready. Approach from the left and
having asked 'May I have your order, sir (madam) please?' wait facing the
guests until (after any advice asked for has been given) the order is completed
as far as and including the main course.

In taking the order observe the following points (Figure 23).

- Face the guests as they make their choice
- Do not stand behind a guest who is ordering

Figure 23 The correct stance of a waiter when taking an order.

- Never lean over the guest nor lean on tables or chairs
- Be ready to deal with queries or to make suggestions
- Be patient with ditherers who are uncertain in choosing
- If guests select a main course only, enquire regarding preliminary course, hors d'oeuvres, appetiser or soup
- Only volunteer suggestions after such time has elapsed that it is apparent they would be welcome

The waiter's order book

Many waiters' books are duplicates. The original is given to the kitchen clerk before he will transmit the order to the chefs concerned. The carbon copy is retained as the waiter's own record (i.e. number and kind of meal served) and may even serve additionally as the bill finally to be presented. Sometimes two carbon copies are made out, the original for the kitchen, one for preparation of the bill and the other for retention by the waiter.

Information required on the order includes:

- the waiter's code number or station number
- the table number
- the number of guests
- the date
- details of dishes
- prices
- the type of meal ordered

If a head waiter records the order, he summons the station waiter and passes over the written order with any verbal instructions.

How to record an order

Write in the corner of the next unused sheet of your order pad the number of the table being served. Then record (using abbreviations) the dishes ordered. Write clearly for it has to be read by others.

Remember the following points.

- Record how guests wish grills, roasts, etc. cooked, that is, blue, rare, well done, etc.
- To avoid confusion or unnecessary further enquiry in serving varied orders, 'identify' guests by using a system of 'invisible' seat numbers and/or brief description notes against order, that is, host, blue frock, moustache, etc.
- Defer taking an order for the sweet or dessert course until the guests have finished the earlier part of the meal
- When orders up to and including the main course have been made, recapitulate them to the guests to ensure accuracy

- Once the order is taken, check again that the table is fully and properly laid so that any necessary action may be taken before service begins

The order for sweets, desserts and cheese are taken in a similar manner when guests have completed their main course.

How to pass the order to the kitchen

You now know the order of service of dishes ordered by your customers. Go (or send your commis) to the kitchen servery, stating the order in a clear voice to the kitchen clerk, or whoever is accepting the orders, and handing over to him your check.

You will then be given the dish. To avoid customers waiting, the first dish on the menu is usually one ready for immediate service, for example, soup or hors d'oeuvre. This will be taken and served immediately, unless the dishes to follow require lengthy preparation. In this case, timing may be adjusted.

Meanwhile, the dishes that are to follow are immediately put into preparation. Fish, poultry or meat may require to be fried, roasted or grilled or cut from the joint. The final course is usually a sweet course from the pastry section of the service table or pastry larder. It may already be prepared (e.g. cold dishes which will need only to be apportioned) or (in high-class restaurants) it may be prepared for each customer and take up to, say, 30 minutes from the time first ordered.

Action after the food order

If the table is laid for service of both soup and hors d'oeuvre or fish and none has been ordered, remove the corresponding silver. When anything on the table is no longer required, remove it on a plate covered with a serviette.

Wine order

Having served aperitifs, the wine winter returns and:

- approaches the host from the left
- presents the wine list
- takes the order, making any necessary suggestions regarding the 'matching' of wine with food and the nature of the wines listed (see Chapter 18 for details of wine service)

Service until departure

Further details of collecting, checking, serving and clearing food and beverages apply up to and including the departure of guests. These are considered in the chapters which follow.

11
Styles of Service

Forms of restaurant service which have evolved such as French, Russian, silver, etc. may be simplified or elaborated in a 'house style' devised to meet the needs of an operation irrespective of tradition. All service forms must relate to the basic reasons for giving service at all, namely to meet consumer requirements and to build food sales through service.

There is evolution in styles rather than revolution; not least because of staff familiarity with established procedures. Such familiarity eases the induction of new staff and helps standardize training both 'on the job' and in training centres.

Aims of service

Style of service should support basic aims of waiting and:

- effectively sell the establishment's food, beverages and service
- attractively present and merchandize saleable commodities and services as an integral 'package'
- help to create a pleasant and appropriate dining atmosphere, especially through welcoming guests

Waiter's role

To achieve the aims of service mentioned above, either in traditional or future forms of service, involves a waiter who:

- communicates guests' requirements to the kitchen and sets in motion action to produce needed dishes
- effects efficient and attractive service of dishes to guests, either in the shortest possible time, or in the time guests deem appropriate
- ensures that orders have been recorded for billing purposes

Principal forms of service

The style of service chosen depends on the restaurant, its ambience, staff employed, its desired speed of guest turnover and other factors.

The style will normally be one of the following (or an adaptation of one of them):

French service (service à la française)
English service (service à l'anglaise)
Family service (plat sur table)
Side-table service (service au guéridon)
Plate service (service à l'assiette or service simplifié)
Russian service (service à la Russe)

General rules

Whatever the style of service, observe the following rules.

• Present all dishes
• Serve all food from the left
• Serve and clear drinks from the right
• Clearance of food plates often is from the left in England, but from the right on the Continent (see p. 113)

Styles and adaptations outlined

Interpretation of how to carry out the various styles and the way they are adapted varies from one country to another (indeed sometimes between different establishments in the same country). In Europe they are generally understood to be as outlined below.

French service

So-called French service in France, Switzerland and elsewhere in Europe is where guests help themselves from a dish placed on the table. Alternatively, the waiter offers the dish for guests to help themselves. This latter also has similarity with the style in private houses where dishes are passed by servants.

1 In France

Basis

The customer helps himself with service spoon and fork from a dish which is offered from the left.

Application

Medium-priced operations, guest houses and, sometimes, functions.

Waiter's action

- Place the dish (with service spoon and fork) on a service cloth folded to form a pad on the palm of the left hand
- Stand near to the guest's left, slightly lean towards him with right hand behind the small of your back and proffer the dish for the guest to serve himself
- Repeat for other guests

Advantages

Relatively few waiters required.
Does not demand high-level skills.

Disadvantages

Slower than waiter serving.
Possible guest uncertainty regarding procedure.

2   In the United Kingdom

Basis

(a) As in France above.
(b) Alternatively, place the main dish on the table
In the case of alternative (b):

Waiter's action (for small parties)

- Optional: place réchaud (perhaps of 'night light' type) on the table before the guest to be served first
- Place the plates before each guest (or alternatively near the réchaud)
- Place the dish with service spoon and fork on the table before the guest (on the réchaud if one is used)

Advantages

Takes less time.
Appreciated by guest.

Disadvantages

Guest clumsiness may cause spillage.

Waiter's action (for larger parties, usually for tables of four or more)

- Use a side-table (guéridon)
- Bring plates and dishes to the guéridon
- Set plates at guests' covers

- Carry out any preliminary treatment (e.g. portioning or carving) on the guéridon
- Present dishes (as in 1 above) for guests' self help

Advantages and disadvantages as for 1 above.

Private house service

This adaptation of style (b) above requires space for dishes of food on guests tables and réchauds for customer self-help. It is normally confined to the main course; other forms of service are usually used for other courses.

Family service

Called in France 'plat sur table' (dish on table), this simplified form of service is used in boarding houses, guest houses and some small institutions. The waiter places the dish (or dishes) on the table for guests to serve themselves.

English service

Basis

Waiters serve each guest and judge portions (as distinct from guests self-help). Guéridon service or service à l'anglaise avec guéridon (see below) is a form of English service. These terms originate in France. Their use has been taught in French and Swiss hotel schools. Some operators in America and Britain are confused by names such as silver service, guéridon or the numbers of waiters involved and this has led to English service being called 'French' service – or at its most refined from the guéridon as 'service à la Ritz'.

Application

Medium- to high-class establishments, banqueting, travel catering, etc.

Waiter's action

Working from the left:

- place a hot or cold plate (as appropriate to the food to be served)
- place the dish on the left palm with the folded service cloth acting as a pad between dish and hand
- lean slightly towards the guest from the left
- with spoon and fork in the right hand, forming, in effect, tongs, serve the food onto the guest's plate

Advantages

Quick and efficient, but still a form of high-class 'silver' service.

Disadvantages

Awkward for serving some fragile foods such as fish and omelets.
Requires some skill and training.
Some risk of spillage on tablecloth or guest clothing.

English service from the guéridon

Mise en place

Assemble service cutlery, the required number of plates and the dishes of
food on the guéridon (a lamp or réchaud is usually also required for the hot
dishes).

Waiter's action

- Effect any carving, filleting or pre-portioning
- Place guest's portion on plate with accompanying garnishes
- Place plates one at a time as completed immediately before guest

(*Note*: guéridon service is facilitated by the use of commis to pass plates)

Advantages

Guests appreciate personal care.
Guests can see what is available and select accordingly.
Guests can see their food completed and express their preference, e.g. portion
size.

Disadvantages

Slow.
Takes more time and staff.
Thus, costs more.

In the previous century in Europe and America, English service was widespread. All dishes to be eaten were placed on the table at the same time and
removed (relieved, relevé) to be replaced by a further assortment. (Hence the
term remove or relevé course which survives.) Thus, the great chef Carême
believed in cooks understanding architecture because elaborate dishes
remained for some time on table display. Principal guests sat before principal
dishes. Guests even took on carving duties. Footmen (forerunners of waiters
in private houses) merely brought in dishes, removed used plates, and filled
and re-filled glasses.

Russian service

The term silver service is applied also to Russian service (and its adaptations)
as outlined below.

In the middle of the nineteenth century, the custom of placing several different dishes on the table and then removing (or 'relieving') them once with another set of dishes went out of fashion. Instead, dining tables were decorated – however, not with food. Servants then brought in and served one course first. Once consumed, this course was cleared. This procedure was repeated course by course. In private houses or clubs, guests helped themselves, but for à la Russe the portion for each person could be clearly distinguished.

For Russian service or service à la Russe in restaurants, waiters presented the dressed dish to guests and then served them. This was once done by making more extensive use of sideboard or side-table for portioning and then distribution of the plates by the waiter or his commis.

Today, 'English' service and 'Russian' service are virtually the same and may both be regarded as standard silver service.

Silver service

French, English and Russian services can also be 'silver' service. But in general, portioning is largely effected in the kitchen so that food, particularly with a varied or complicated garnish, may easily be separated and served by the waiter.

Silver service normally implies that the waiter brings plates and dishes to the sideboard, places a plate before each guest at his own cover, presents the main dish to the host or guest and then passes round the table serving each customer. But as noted above, this form of service also can be (and in high-grade establishments is) effected from the guéridon.

Each waiter should serve no fewer than a station of 12 guests.

Basis

1 Service by waiters using spoon and fork in one hand from silver or similar dishes.
2 Service from side-table, guéridon or serving trolleys.

Application

Medium to high class establishments, banquets, travel catering, etc.

Waiter's action

As for English service 1 and 2 previously.

Advantages and Disadvantages

As for English service 1 and 2 previously.

Semi-silver service

English, French, Russian and 'silver' services generally may be adapted in various ways. Two main variants yield a 'semi-silver service'.

- Plate the main items (meat, poultry, game or fish), but also serve from silver such accompaniments as sauces and/or vegetables
- Serve main items from silver, but place on the table for guest self-service sauces and/or vegetables

Each waiter should serve no fewer than a station of 18 guests.

Guéridon service

As indicated above, 'silver' service or English service may be done from a guéridon or side-table. In advanced forms of service from the guéridon in luxury restaurants, additional processes involving waiting craft skills have to be mastered. This treatment is further considered in Chapter 15.

Staffing is similar to silver service.

Plate service

Plate service is broadly of two types:

> up-market: where the kitchen chef seeks to present food dressed as he intends it to look and taste
> popular: when the customer is served in a simple manner

Each waiter should be able to servce a station of not less than 24 guests.

Basis

In both cases, to present the guest with his food ready served in the kitchen, servery or buffet onto the plate.

Application

Up-market: high-class restaurants or more modest priced 'serious' operations where the chef seeks to present food as quickly as possible after cooking and arranged to show his craft skill and artistry.

Popular: canteens, guest/boarding houses and restaurants seeking fast service.

Waiter's action

In cafeteria services or from buffet, plated dishes are collected by guests and waiting service is eliminated or confined to clearing.

In 'serious' restaurants:

- the waiter takes plates covered with dish covers to restaurant

either

- removes cover at sideboard and, from the left, places plate before guest with the meat, poultry, game or fish portion nearest to him at the '6 o'clock' position and with the crest or badge at the top or '12 o'clock' position *or*

- from the left, places the covered plate before the guest and removes the cover; immediately reversing the cover so that any moisture is retrieved inside the cover.

Advantages

Speed, minimal equipment, standardized presentation
Chef's concept of dish is presented direct
Aids portion control
Fewer waiting staff required

Disadvantages

Vigilance needed to ensure hot food remains hot
Many customers like to be served

Note

Accompaniments such as potato, noodles or rice may be passed or offered separately in some establishments.

American service

This form of service also depends on pre-plating and pre-setting of the table with cutlery and in many cases (e.g. banquets) with coffee cups and saucers needed throughout the meal. American style in older textbooks is scarcely mentioned for its influence has only gradually and relatively recently become apparent internationally. In America, service has been conditioned by the need to make effective use of labour and reflects a 'rationalization' of waiting techniques. American service may not yet have reached its final form, but for ordinary restaurants usually requires:

- a simple form of guéridon (often a large tray on a collapsable stand) or trolley to convey plated food from the servery to the guest's table
- plated food then passed to the guest

In up-market establishments, the semblance of guéridon service is supported by carts or trolleys for special services from containers carried by waiting staff; and by the use of table equipment and appointments of fine quality. Thus, whilst service may be simplified, the illusion of personal 'guéridon service' and high quality may be heightened.

Staffing for service

In traditional, high-class restaurants, a brigade of waiters is organized on the basic idea that one waiter (the 'chef de rang' or station waiter) is in charge of four, five, six or more tables with assistance from one or more 'commis'. This is to carry out any silver service, English or French style (especially English silver service) from the guéridon. With commis to bring dishes from the kitchen and to do the 'fetching and carrying', the chef de rang waiter can attend to finer points of actual service to the guest. Otherwise, for basic silver service about 12 guests per waiter is average; increasing to about 18 guests for modified or semi-silver service. For basic service (such as popular plate presentation), about 24 guests per waiter is average, but the proportion may be varied according to menu, speed of guest turnover, and other factors.

12

Sequence, Technique and Tools

Once you have taken guests' orders you will have to attend to several customers and tables at one time. You must cultivate your memory and skills to obtain and serve the various dishes promptly and correctly.

Coordinating orders

Bear in mind the following points.

- After serving one course, go to the kitchen for the next. Bring this to the side-table in time to take away customers' used plates and to serve the next course
- Check other tables at your station before leaving the restaurant for the kitchen area to ensure that no other guests seek your attention
- Each course takes time to be eaten, so you have 5–10 minutes to serve a course to other guests. You may have 16 or more customers at any one time during service. Some customers will be at the first stage, others at the second stage, and yet others at the third or final course. Coordinate your journey to the kitchen to obtain the next courses which are required for each of these
- If there is any delay in obtaining an order, the customer must be informed by the head waiter who will offer regrets and a suitable excuse

Order of service

- In a party of *two*, a lady and gentleman, serve the lady first
- In a party of four, two ladies and two gentlemen, serve the lady on the right of the host first, then the lady on his left, the gentleman opposite the host and finally the host
- In a party of six, three ladies and three gentlemen, the host and hostess sit facing each other. Serve the lady on the right of the host first, followed by the lady on the left, then the hostess. Next serve the gentle-

man on the right of the hostess, then the one on the left of the hostess and, finally, the host

- In a large party but with a host rather than a chairman, the guest of honour, who is sitting on the right of the host, is served first (in a mixed party this is usually a lady), then the guest on his left, then the host himself. The other waiter on the top table of a large party starts with the first guest on the right of the guest of honour. (For order of function service see Chapter 20)
- In a smaller party with a host, serve the lady on the right of the host first, then the lady on his left. Then continue round the table to the right regardless of sex, serving the host last

Techniques

During meal service there are many points to observe concerning the service of different courses, salads and accompaniments and some special dishes.* A waiter must master a number of techniques involving a variety of tools and equipment.

Sideboard work

The dining table is the focal point of a waiter's work and guests' enjoyment; whereas the sideboard or side-table is the waiter's work bench. 'Sidework' as it is called in USA (though in America this term extends to ménage work generally), plays a key role in supporting service to guests.

Preparation of the sideboard has already been described (see Chapter 9). Points to be remembered when using the sideboard are as follows:

- Do not allow sideboard activity to dominate all other activities
- Leaving sideboard work to attend to a guest is not an 'interruption' Guests come first. Sideboard and other work supports and leads to such service
- Make an efficient work point by keeping your sideboard clear and clean and adequately stocked
- Replenish items as they are used during service
- Stock sideboard adequately

Basic service tools

A waiter uses far fewer hand tools than the kitchen chef, generally only the cutlery normally found in a dining room.

---

* For advanced techniques in guéridon service, carving, salad and dressing making and flambé work, the reader is referred to John Fuller's *Guéridon and Lamp Cookery, 2nd edition* published by Hutchinson, 1979).

A waiter's prime tools are:

service spoon and fork
service salver
service cloth
dishes on which the food is presented

In special services a waiter uses carving tools (most frequently a sharpened table knife and fork or a fish knife and fork), lamps, chafing dishes and the appliances linked with them.

Some people contend that tongs, tweezers or slices (such as those used for gâteaux) could be more extensively employed in service; rather than reliance on the manipulation by a waiter of spoon and fork or two forks. However, this manipulation is easier than it looks. It can be mastered within minutes, and proficiency achieved within hours. This simple skill prevents increasing the number of tools in a restaurant, thus keeping inventories as simple as possible.

Service spoon and fork

From the guéridon: service spoon held in the right hand and fork in the left hand; employed in such a straightforward manner as to require little handling instruction.

In silver services: service spoon and fork must be used with one hand because the other holds the dish (Figure 24).

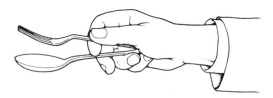

Figure 24   Service spoon and fork.

Using service spoon and fork in one hand enables these two items to act as tongs; a finger is a lever so that the fork prongs and spoon bowl may be opened and closed to hold food items securely. To do this:

- lay the service spoon bowl uppermost on the table
- place on it the service fork so that the curve of the fork prongs fits into the bowl making spoon and fork virtually parallel
- take up the two items together so that the palm of the hand and all the fingers are over both handles
- Hold the two together, obtaining a comfortable balance, then insert the first finger midway between the spoon and fork handles

Spoon and fork together are now supported by the fifth (the little finger) and fourth and third fingers. The spoon is primarily supported by the third finger. The first (forefinger) supports the fork which is also pinioned gently by the thumb. This makes the first and forefinger a lever. Practice opening and closing the spoon and fork 'pincer' thus formed. With the handles comfortably centred in the palm you can lock the spoon and fork in any position.

Beginners may practice lifting any objects (dried peas, even pieces of paper) from table surfaces before they progress to actual food items.

To use the spoon and fork 'lever' for rounded objects such as bread rolls or potatoes, reverse the serving fork so that the curve of the prongs form an oval shape with the bowl of the spoon. Opening and closing technique remains the same.

Points in using the serving spoon and fork as a service tool (Figure 25)

- The spoon part performs the major role
- In lifting an item from a serving dish, insert the spoon gently under the item; only when the spoon is underneath should you lever the fork down to hold the food item firmly but gently
- Do not grab at the food in a claw-like fashion from the outset; the fork is merely the steadying part. Though forming a pincer with the spoon, it is not a 'grabbing pincer'. 'Grabbing' can damage food, particularly delicate items.

Figure 25   Using the service spoon and fork.

Service spoon alone

Beginners, delighted with their mastery of spoon and fork techniques, may abuse it rather than use it. For example, they use the two implements together when a spoon alone would be more effective; as in the service of vegetables such as peas and potato purée.

When food may be neatly served with a spoon alone, then use it alone; the simplest tool is normally the best and avoids unnecessary soiling of cutlery.

Splaying technique

A thin, flat item of food such as a fillet of sole may be hard to transfer without breaking with a spoon and fork used in the normal lever fashion from service dish to plate. In such cases, splay your service implements.

For food of this kind, two forks may be more efficient than a spoon and fork.

- Place the two forks in your palm, but do not lever by inserting your forefinger
- Instead, fan them out to open sideways at an angle of anything up to 90°, but usually about 45°, so that the forks provide a platform
- Both forks may now be inserted gently and simultaneously underneath the food to be lifted from service dish to guest's plate

Some traditionalist waiters are against using anything other than a spoon and fork but where two splayed forks will do the job better, then use them. When sauce or gravy is present, have a spoon also on the dish.

Changing service cutlery

Use clean service implements for each different service of food; particularly when serving vegetables after a meat or fish course. Then use separate serving implements for each different type of vegetable.

This does not apply to a garnished entrée where you use the same implements to serve everything on the dish. However, if, for example, spinach à la crème and boiled potatoes are presented simultaneously, use different service gear for each. Similarly, have different sets of service gear on a tray or trolley of hors d'oeuvre.

Service gear check points

The following summarizes the procedure in using service implements.

- Use clean service implements for each dish
- Never use them again for service at another table
- Do not use the same service implements for different types of vegetables even when presented simultaneously
- Splay service spoon and fork or two forks for large, flat items such as omelets and fish fillets
- Where a fish or similar item is still too large for service even with splayed implements, divide it across the middle with service spoon
- Two forks may be employed (in the case of omelets and fish fillets), but it is not customary to use two spoons
- When food (e.g. large omelets) have to be divided and have been presented to the host, ensure that you mentally calculate portion size before again approaching the table to serve

Ladles and spoons

Ladles are not regarded as hand tools in the same way as service spoons and forks.

For clear gravy or only slightly thickened sauce, use a small sauce ladle.

For thick sauces (e.g. Béarnaise), choose a spoon rather than a ladle. It is less likely to clog and make service difficult.

Service cloth

The service cloth is an important tool of your trade because you carry it constantly during service and use it in a variety of ways for a variety of tasks. Ensure that it is clean and used only to aid in service, for example to handle cutlery and crockery (Figure 26) or act as a pad in handling hot dishes; it should never be used as a duster, a 'flicker' or a swab.

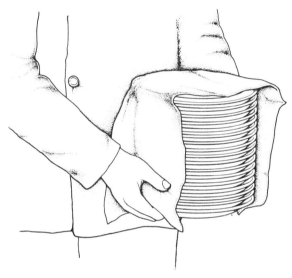

Figure 26 The service cloth can be used in a variety of ways, for example when carrying a pile of plates.

Never use a table napkin as a substitute for a service cloth. Under no circumstances employ for any purpose whatsoever a napkin used by a guest, but put it for laundering immediately.

Use the service cloth as follows:

During table laying and preparation: to 'finish' cutlery, glasses and other table items with a final polish, but it is not a duster nor swab, never use it to dust furniture or wipe table and other surfaces.

During service: it enables you to handle service dishes, that is, to insulate your hands against heat and/or to steady items and to prevent rattling.

When handling a hot service dish: fold it neatly into a pad to form a flat, secure cushion between your palm and the underside of the dish. Even for cold dishes, this technique is desirable for steadiness.

When not in use, to hold dishes: carry your service cloth neatly folded on your left forearm; never tucked between your upper forearm and body into the armpit. It is unhygienic and extremely distasteful to guests.

Crumbing down: use a clean napkin for crumbing down tables; not a service cloth.

Polishing: before placing plates at the cover, wipe their undersides with your service cloth (ring marks of dirt or moisture can occur even with satisfactory washing-up arrangements). The top of plates should not require polishing; reject them if they are not clean (a service cloth constantly handled by the waiter is not appropriate for polishing during service periods; though the clean one is so used during mise en place time).

Finally, a service cloth should be clean and look clean at all times; change it as necessary during service for it should never have a soiled, limp or used appearance.

Carried kit

Apart from your serving equipment, always carry:

- a pencil (or ball point pen) for checking
- a corkscrew and bottle opener (even if you are not on wine waiting duties this may be required in emergencies)
- a cigar cutter, matches or gas lighter (if allowed by management)

Equipment usage: checklist

- Check dishes, glasses, cutlery and all table equipment for cleanliness before they enter the restaurant and before use. Cracks and chips are dangerous as well as unsightly for they harbour bacteria. Reject them. Good management will dispose of them as rubbish immediately
- Wipe rims of service dishes as required
- Return anything dropped on the floor (cutlery, plates and, of course, food) by taking it on tray or plate to the service area for washing (in the case of cutlery, crockery, etc.) or refuse (if food)
- Keep sideboards clean and uncluttered
- Restaurant ware such as cutlery, crockery and glasses have a guest's part and a waiter's part. Handle only *your* part, especially:
  cups, jugs, etc.   — by handle only (never rims, never gather together several cups by hand spreadeagled in the rim)

knives, forks, spoons, etc. – by handle only (never by blades, prongs or bowls). Never carry cutlery by stacking in cups or jugs

glasses   – by stems (or foot in case of tumblers) and never rims

• Use napkin-covered plate or salver to convey cutlery from sideboard to guest's table

Rules of serving

All styles of service are conditioned by general rules of serving. The following outlines basic procedures used in silver service and generally in good waiting.

Sides of service

On which side of the guest a waiter works is important only in that it is:

> *efficient*: for example, as guests' drinking glasses are on the right hand side, serving wine (or other beverages) from the right is logical
> *familiar*: guests become used to waiters approaches and should not be 'surprised' by method

Thus, each establishment should be consistent in what is practiced.

Continental practice

An indication is given at relevant points in this book of whether plate placing, service or clearing should be from the right or left. Rules of the continental tradition may be summarized as below.

• Place clean plates and glasses from the guest's right
• Place coffee cups and saucers (with underplate) from the guest's left
• Serve food from the left
• Serve drinks (including wines and coffee) from the right
• Clear used items (plates, cups and glasses) from the right

The above is observed in most establishments in Europe, particularly France and Switzerland, and is the basis of teaching in most continental hotel schools.

Adaptations

In many restaurants and training centres in Britain, this European mode is adapted, particularly in regard to clearance, and either right or left hand clearance may be regarded as correct. However, always follow the 'house' rules of any particular restaurant as to the side for clearance adopted; however once a decision is taken, the observance of it should be total. Never mix right and left hand clearance in any one restaurant (except when, as noted below, guests convenience is involved). For example:

> do not interrupt a conversation in order to serve
> do not force your way between the wall and the back of the customer's chair

Beverage serving

Serve drinks from the right (but further detail regarding wine service may be found in Chapter 18). Place coffee cups and sugar (unless it is on the same salver as the coffee) from the left. Coffee, as other beverages, is served from the right.

Bread serving

Place or offer bread to the guest from the left.

Service and clearance sides summarized

The foregoing notes may be summarized as:

Continental tradition: serve food from left
serve liquids from right
clear from right

British adaptation: serve food from left
clear food from left
serve liquids from right
clear liquids from right

Serving from silver

When as a waiter you bring food already dressed on a silver dish, observe the following.

Presentation: present the dish to the host for his approval before serving guests and to show it is what he ordered
place a spoon and fork on the dish for service
Stance: stand on the left, feet together
hold the dish on the palm of your left hand, which is protected by your folded waiter's cloth
bend (advancing your left foot forward) to bring the dish down to the plate just over the rim; the dish being perfectly level
with your right hand take the spoon and fork to serve food on to the plate in the 'claw' manner described above.
Once presented, all portioning must be done within view of guests.

Arranging: arrange food neatly and carefully (do not allow the portion to slide off) onto the guest's plate: the main item (fish, poultry or game) lower centre; vegetables to one side and potatoes on the other. Seek to reproduce the chef's lay-out of accompaniments on the silver dish in *your* plate arrangement.

Service reminders: ensure that the serving spoon and fork for each dish are clean; for example, do not use the same spoon and fork for both potatoes and green vegetables.

- Do not re-use a fork and spoon on one table after it has been used at another
- Never use two spoons
- Do not use a fork without a spoon (except in rare instances, i.e. in serving smoked salmon, cucumber salad)
- If a fish portion is too big for easy service with the spoon and fork, sever it across the middle with the spoon
- When serving an omelet, cut off the extreme tips with the spoon before serving. (Two fork serving is acceptable for certain omelets fourées)
- If an omelet (or other item) has to be cut into several portions, check exactly how many beforehand to avoid unequal portioning
- For dessert service if the dessert spoon and fork are placed across the top of the cover move them down to the right and left of the cover

Service from the guéridon

See Chapter 15.

Putting on plates (silver service)

Temperature and cleanliness of plates are vital. For hot courses they must be hot; for cold courses, cold. However, hot plates should not be so hot that they cannot be handled.

- Hold the pile of plates on your left hand (not between thumb and fingers) which should be covered with one end of your waiter's cloth
- On approaching the right (or left, see final sentence of this paragraph) of the customer, wipe the top plate gently with the other end of the cloth, then pick up the plate with the tips of the thumb and fingers of the right hand
- Keeping the plate horizontal, lower it into position
- Repeat round the table, finishing with the host
- Check the cleanliness of plates before they reach the table, rather than having to wipe them in front of the guest (though wiping the underside before placing is prudent)
- Plates are usually placed from the guest's right side in continental styles of service, but in Britain there is a slight bias in favour of placing from the guest's left

Removing plates

You may clear used plates either from the left or the right hand side of the customer, according to the rule of the establishment (but the whole room must work in the same way).

- Remove the used plates directly everyone in the party has finished (but not before), leaving the host until last.
- Give priority in clearing plates, first to keep the table tidy and, second, to prevent the customer from feeling that he is being forgotten

The correct method of removing plates with cutlery is as follows.

- Pick up the plates with your right hand and transfer them to the left
- Hold the first plate by the thumb lying along the edge of the plate pointing across the body, and the first two fingers underneath, slightly spread. Your third and fourth fingers stand up outside the plate, the tips level with the thumb (Figure 27)
- Place the used fork with the curve upwards

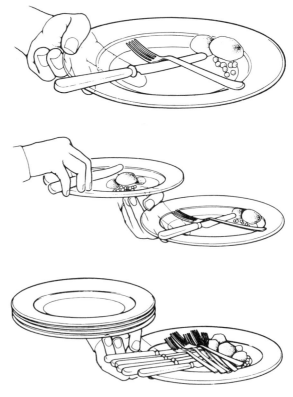

Figure 27 The correct method of clearing plates.

- Place the used knife under the curve of the fork and at right-angles (this is the technique known as the 'first plate')
- Place the second plate on your forearm with the under rim behind the thumb joint and on the two extended fingers. In this way the plate cannot slip forward and the main weight is supported by the forearm (Figure 27)
- Now pick up the knife and fork and gently scrape any remains of food onto the first plate
- Then place them with the other cutlery on the first plate, fork with fork, knife under the forks, as before
- Continue round the table in this manner until it is cleared
- You should be able to clear eight places comfortably in this fashion

Points to note

- By using this method you have a neat stack of plates which do not wobble and are not top-heavy
- When you go to the side-table you can take the first plate out of your left hand (using your right hand to do so) and place it on the top of the pile so that the whole pile is completely steady
- Shifting food from one plate to the other should be done, as far as possible, out of guests' vision
- The angle of the cutlery on the first plate should be such that should anything fall, it will do so towards the waiter and not the customer
- Pick up immediately any article of silver dropped on the floor and take it to the sideboard. Never use it at the table
- Never put back on the dish any food dropped on the floor. Pick it up immediately, put on a plate and take it out of the restaurant. (Do this with delicacy, for example, use a discarded menu as a scoop in such a way as to make clear that the dropped food will be thrown away. This is important as the customer is likely to be watching)
- Carry clean cups, glasses, etc. on a salver and lift them by their handles or stems and never by putting your fingers inside them
- Remove dirty glasses by means of a salver and not by hand
- Handle dishes, plates and cutlery as silently as possible
- Do not allow glasses to knock against one another as this makes an unpleasant noise. (Some guests may even have superstitions about this)

13

Coping During Service

The general progress of a meal is predictable, but a waiter must be both aware of routine and ready to deal with the unexpected.

Meal service routine

As a meal progresses, a waiter should at all times know what he is supposed to be doing. Points to observe are listed below.

- Ensure that the wine waiter has attended to your guest and that the wine to accompany food is ready for service with the appropriate course
- Estimate the time it will take for you to serve, and for guests to consume, courses throughout your section. Be familiar with food preparation times; to ensure that tables are served appropriately staggered to minimize delays and aid smoothness

   Thus, keep in mind the timing of courses and order to time courses which are to follow.
- Serve the first course as quickly as possible to start, but if cooking time will delay the service of the main course to follow, arrange first course service so that the interval between courses is not unduly prolonged
- Serve dishes immediately they arrive at the station from the kitchen; never allow them to lie on the sideboard
- Check tables constantly to ensure that guests have appropriate cutlery, cruet, accompaniments for food, wine and water glasses replenished, ' butter adequate and bread passed as required
- When serving make sure that portioning is equitable, hot dishes are hot (and served on hot plates) and that all is scrupulously clean
- Take the order for sweet or dessert promptly after the clearance of the main course saying 'what will you have to follow, sir. May I show you the sweet trolley?' (Guests who light cigarettes after the main course prompt the waiter to proceed to sweet service)
- Suggest coffee and have the wine waiter (or cigar and liqueur trolley) attend the table to offer brandy, liqueur and cigars

Courtesy and attentiveness

Courtesy should result from instinctively good mannered attentiveness. The following points exemplify this approach.

- Anticipate guests' requirements including special condiments, sideboard sauces for appropriate dishes, a light for a cigarette
- Ensure that guests have no difficulty in 'catching your eye'. Watch for a turned head, it usually means a guest requires service
- Request guests' permission if you wish to remove an item (such as sugar sifter, cruet) for another table's use
- Remove nothing from the guest's place, glass, dish, etc. until you are certain he has finished. Normally this is signalled by the guest placing knife and fork (spoon and fork) neatly together across the centre of the plate (12 o'clock to 6 o'clock position)
- Do not remove a dish because a guest is absorbed in conversation and seems to ignore his plate
- However, be vigilant in the case of those who have indicated that they are in a hurry. In such circumstances you may ask if a guest has finished

Checkpoints in serving techniques

- When you have to serve some customers with hot and others with cold dishes, serve the cold dishes first
- Always remove crumbs and bread from the table before serving the sweet or dessert course. (For this 'crumbing down' use a neatly folded table napkin as a brush to bring the crumbs to the edge of the table. From the edge bring them gently onto a medium-sized plate)
- Remove the cruet from the table at the end of the meat course, just before the sweet is served
- If a finger bowl is served, place it on the left of the customer; if it is served at the end of the meal, place it in front of him, after the dessert dish has been removed
- Never lay a chipped glass or plate, and avoid serving from any such imperfect article
- Anything dropped to the floor should be taken to the side-table for replacement — not only food, but any article (serviette, knife, etc.) dropped
- Do not keep articles such as teaspoons, menu cards or sugar lumps in your pocket. (The menu card should be on the table or the side-table, never tucked inside your shirt front)
- When serving food in containers (e.g. grapefruit or ice cream in coupes), place a doyley and an underplate under the container
- When serving a beverage, keep the handle of the jug or pot away from the customer, but turn the handle of the cup, etc. from which he will

drink to his right. (This is why beverage, including coffee, service is always from the right)

- Place sugar, cream, etc. at the customer's right within easy reach
- Make sure during service that all dishes are completely served, that is that all sauces and condiments required are passed with the dish and that the customer has the correct cutlery
- Train yourself to notice right away whether anything is missing from the table
- Check that the customer can reach required items like salt and pepper
- Observe whether the butter dish contains butter
- Remember to pass rolls again during the meal each time a guest has finished the one on his plate or that the plate or dish containing toast Melba is never empty

These exemplify, rather than exhaust, points a waiter watches.

Possible problems

Types of customer, especially in moderately priced and busy establishments, who may create problems include:

Guests in a hurry   Suggest any 'quick service' room or counter if available. Otherwise give guests an accurate appreciation of service time, steer guests away from 'slow dishes' (long preparation and/or elaborate service) and give good service compatible with speed.

Drunk guests and eccentrics   Report signs of drunkenness or oddity to management, who must decide whether to withhold service. Otherwise be tactful, quietly spoken and serve expeditiously. Refer to management any sign of 'trouble', bad language or behaviour.

Flirtatious guests (or 'familiar' behaviour)   Waitresses may have to cope with the 'ladykiller'. Treat familiarity with quick service and refer real difficulties to supervisor. Waiters, similarly, should not respond to over-familiarity.

Solitary diner   The guest alone may be especially observant and critical. Seat him where he can see the restaurant and guest activity generally, to avoid his over-preoccupation with his own service. Avoid drawing attention to his being alone by the direct question prior to seating, that is, do not ask 'Are you alone, sir?'

Children   Help with suggestions for suitable dishes. Deviate from conventional place settings as necessary, for example, to provide a handled drinking vessel. Do not allow children to move around the restaurant or bang table tops and courteously explain the reasons to parents.

Grumblers and trouble-makers   Greet an ill-humoured guest with quiet and good-humoured courtesy. Careful attention and good food may revive his spirits. Do not respond to an argumentative guest with argument and do not identify with the grumbler in any criticism he makes of other colleagues or management.

Animals   Dogs (and other animals) are not usually allowed inside good-class restaurants; however, dealing with the guest who wants his dog in the dining room demands courtesy and tact as well as firmness, and may require referral to the head waiter.

Accident reports and action

Mishaps can occur to guests and their belongings despite waiting staff care. Food and drink may be spilled and spot guests' clothing; stockings may be laddered on a chair and so on. Some incidents may result in claims by guests for compensation and for management to refer to their insurance company. Hence, a restaurant should have report forms to record time, place and circumstances of accidents, names of staff involved and full particulars (name and address) of guests concerned. Thus, follow house procedures such as those listed below.

- Report *at once* mishaps of any kind to the head waiter
- Avoid comment on an accident in front of guests
- Be aware of which staff members are trained in first aid so that appropriate aid may be summoned
- Do not attempt first aid in ignorance and avoid moving any one who seems seriously ill or injured
- Hand any guests' belongings left behind to the lost property section (or head waiter or cashier desk)

Spills and stains

Attend immediately to anything spilled on the table or floor.

- Scoop onto a clean plate with a table knife or spoon any soiled matter dropped on the table
- For damp stains, slip a clean piece of card (such as a white menu) under the cloth, then cover the area of the stain with a clean napkin
- For an extensively stained area, a napperon may be needed to re-cover the entire surface
- Immediately bring a clean napkin and a jug of hot water when anything is spilled onto guests' clothing for damp sponging (then follow the procedure for reporting accidents)
- Scoop up straight away food spilled onto the floor and remove quickly from the restaurant

- Wipe away stains on the floor, either from food or liquids, with a damp cloth

Positive approach to problems

Apart from mishaps and 'problem people', complaints may arise from other food and service causes. Your work aim is to *prevent* any cause for complaint. To this end serve food and wine with care.

- Check each dish for cleanliness and appearance before presentation
- When serving do not 'overload' plates; but return to the table with service dishes as necessary to replenish
- Do not overfill glasses
- Never touch food (e.g. bread rolls) with hands
- Draw the attention of your supervisor to any unsatisfactory feature or dish (portion size, quality, etc.)
- Ensure that any dish sold out is removed from the menu immediately (guest irritation may escalate in other directions)

Satisfying complainants

Management wish to be aware of complaints and their causes so as to apologize and take action as necessary, to remedy faults and prevent recurrence.

- Be ready, therefore, to transmit complaints from guests to supervisors (e.g. head waiters), who in turn inform management
- Strive to avoid causes for complaint but if a fault evokes complaint (rather than endured silently), remedial action (courteous apology and swift corrective action) can be taken
- If a guest does select an item that is 'off', adequately apologize and suggest a substitute
- Apologize for, and attempt to explain, any unavoidable delay (without implying criticism of the kitchen or others)
- Remember when poor quality or service is complained of, a supervisor or manager should respond
- The slogan the 'guest is always right' remains a useful guide; for argument is seldom constructive. Even if the guest *is* wrong, it is unhelpful to cause him to 'lose face' by proving him wrong; not if you wish his custom (and perhaps that of his friends) again
- In avoiding any suggestion of dispute with guests, always refer difficulties to the head waiter if you cannot courteously remedy them
- Be patient, polite and helpful with 'difficult' guests; do not allow them to disconcert you
- Finally, always refer to a supervisor problems that are beyond your capacity to remedy

14
Serving Courses and Dishes

Many techniques of service depend upon product knowledge, that is knowledge of food and its cooking (see Chapters 2, 3 and 4). Waiters must understand the sequence of courses, the dishes that comprise each course and how to serve them.

Accompaniments

Many dishes have separate accompaniments and as they are not always mentioned on the menu, you should know them. Points to remember are:

- hot adjuncts accompany the dish from the kitchen
- cold sauces may often be on the buffet or sideboard
- have accompaniments ready for service with the dish to which they belong

Except in certain instances, specified later:

- serve accompaniments from the guest's left on to the top right of his plate (not on the rim)
- carry a sauceboat on an underdish or small plate on the palm of your left hand, adopting the same stance as for a main dish. Point the sauceboat lip towards the guest's plate. Pass the spoon or ladle over the lip. Do not pour from a boat.

Examples of dishes, accompaniments and cooking times are noted below and French words for main items follow the English to aid menu recognition.

Hors d'oeuvre varié

Cover: Fish knife and fork (or meat knife and fork).
Accompaniments: oil and vinegar cruet on the table before serving.

Hors d'oeuvre varié should be presented on a trolley, each variety in a 'ravier' or similar dish.

- Use separate servers (spoons, fork) for each variety
- Wheel the trolley to the customers' table, near the person to be served
- Remove the hors d'oeuvre plate (fish plate) from the right hand side of the customer with your right hand and place in your left hand
- Use your service cloth to hold this plate while serving from raviers according to the customer's instruction
- When service is completed, place the plate before the customer from the left
- Then wheel the trolley to the next person to be served
- Repeat the routine until all guests have been served

On certain occasions, a special tray or dish containing several compartments may be carried by the waiter to serve hors d'oeuvre.

- A separate item is placed in each compartment with its own servers
- Serve from the dish directly onto the plate in front of the customer, revolving your dish on your hand until you have offered each variety

Single hors d'oeuvre

The following 'single' items are also served as opening courses.

Caviar

Cover: a fish plate and a side knife (or caviar knife if available), a finger bowl, a pepper mill and cayenne pepper.
   Caviar is usually offered in the original container buried in a silver timbale filled with crushed ice and served with a dessert spoon.

Accompaniments: pass blinis, a type of hot pancake or, alternatively, hot toast (breakfast thickness) and slices of brown bread; also half lemons in muslin, finely chopped onions and chopped parsley and, in some restaurants, sieved egg white and yolk.

Oysters (huitres)

Cover: an oyster fork across the tip of the joint knife at an angle of 45°.
   Serve oysters on a special oyster plate or on a round silver flat or a soup plate (if individual portion) covered with broken ice.

Accompaniments: place on the table between two guests: an oyster cruet consisting of chili vinegar, Tobasco sauce, a pepper mill and cayenne pepper (or pass these). Offer brown bread and butter or thin brown bread and butter sandwiches with the oysters. Have at hand plain or other vinegars in case requested by guests. Lemon is essential; normally serve half a lemon per portion.

As the guest finishes: place a finger bowl, half filled with tepid water on a side plate covered with a small napkin and serve to him, set a little to the left of the cover.

Seafood cocktails

Made with one main ingredient such as prawn, shrimp, lobster or crab or mixed sea food (fruits de mer), served in a coupe (silver or glass) on a side plate.

Cover: a teaspoon and oyster or fish fork.

Accompaniment: buttered brown bread, pepper mill and cayenne pepper are offered.

Smoked fish (e.g. eel, mackerel, trout)

Cover: fish knife and fork; serve on a fish plate.

Accompaniments: buttered brown bread, peppers (mill and cayenne), lemon wedge. Horseradish sauce offered, especially with smoked eel.

Smoked salmon (saumon fumé)

Cover: a fish knife and fork (Figure 28).

Smoked salmon is usually cut in very thin slices in the dining room in front of the guest and placed directly on the plate. For functions, it is cut in the kitchen and the slices arranged on a silver flat, then served with a fork only, rolling the slivers round the prongs and unfolding them onto the guest's plate.

Figure 28   A fish cover: for fish-based hors d'oeuvre or fish course.

Accompaniments: on the table, pepper mill, cayenne pepper and a bottle of chili vinegar. Half lemons wrapped in muslin and buttered brown bread, with the crusts removed, are offered.

Terrine de pâté de foie gras

Cover: entrée plate and side knife.

Mise en place: a jug of hot water and dessert spoon.

- Present the pate in its original container (terrine) buried in a bed of crushed ice
- Dip the spoon into hot water and scoop a portion (roughly a spoonful) from the terrine with the spoon and put it on the entrée plate
- Dip the spoon again into hot water before serving the next guest

Accompaniments: Hot brioche and/or hot toast (trimmed of crust and slightly thinner than for breakfast service) with fresh butter separately.

Accompaniments for other single hors d'oeuvres

Plover (or gulls') eggs (oeufs de pluvier)

- Cut brown bread and butter
- Spiced (oriental) salt
- Finger bowl

Potted shrimps

- Cut brown bread and butter (alternatively hot toast)
- Cayenne pepper, pepper mill, lemon

Snails (Escargots)

Cover: Snail fork and tongs (Figure 29). Serve hot on snail dish on underplate (Figure 30).

Accompaniments: French bread (offered).

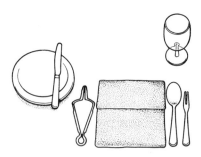

Figure 29 An escargot cover.

Figure 30 An escargot dish.

Juices

Tomato juice (jus de tomate)

● Worcestershire sauce on table (teaspoon for stirring)

Fruit juices

● Caster sugar sifter (or similar dispenser) available

Fruit appetizers

Avocado pear
Cover: teaspoon and dessert fork. Serve in shaped avocado dish (Figure 31) or on small (fish) plate.

Figure 31 An avocado dish.

Accompaniment: vinaigrette (offered).

Grapefruit (pamplemousse)
Always prepared before service, usually by the waiting staff.

● Halve against the segment
● Cut each segment of the flesh separately

- Decorate with a cocktail cherry (usually)
- Set in a silver grapefruit cup, placed on an entrée plate with a teaspoon alongside the cup
- Serve from the left

Accompaniments: pass fine caster sugar immediately the grapefruit is served; leave on the table. set a finger bowl afterwards.

Fruit cocktail (cocktail de fruit)

Serve fruit cocktail similarly, either in cocktail coupes or in glasses. Finger bowls are not needed.

Melon (melon and canteloupe)

Two kinds of melon are frequently served; canteloupe, a yellow-skinned, gourd-like melon and honeydew, larger and usually greener, of Rugby football shape.

Cover: a melon (fruit) knife and fork placed across the plate, the tip of the knife handle resting on the fork prongs.

Optional addition: a dessert spoon laid across the plate with its handle to the right.

- Normally place the slice of melon on the plate at the sideboard, in the space between the crossed knife and fork
- then place it in front of the guest.

Accompaniments:

- Place a sugar dredger on the table
- Pass a silver flat with two bowls, one with caster sugar and one with ground ginger
- Place a couple of teaspoons of sugar neatly on the side of the guest's plate and a smaller quantity of ginger alongside it, as may be requested
- Do not sprinkle sugar (or ginger) over the melon

Melon, usually an hors d'oeuvre, can be served as a sweet.

Parma ham is sometimes served with honeydew melon. Melon, especially canteloupe, is often made into a melon cocktail, flavoured with port or other wine.

Soup (Potage)

Thick soup, from tureen

When serving soup (normally from the sideboard) use an underlayer plate.

- Hold the underplate in your left hand, place the soup plate on it and then serve the soup from the tureen using a silver soup ladle

- Should any soup be spilled on the soup plate's edge, wipe it with the service cloth before serving the customer (from his left)
- When removing soup plates, lift both plates at once

Soup from individual bowls
Alternatively, individual portions can be presented in silver soup bowls.

- Set soup plate and underplate before the guest
- From the left, carefully tilt the silver bowl to transfer the soup, away from the guest, into the bowl

Soup is also often served from a guéridon placed near the customers' table. A spirit lamp may be used to keep soup hot while it is being served; but take care not to over-heat certain thick soups as they may 'turn' or curdle if boiled.

Clear soup (consommé)
Consommé is usually served in consommé cups, that is, cups with two handles. The complete set consists of an entrée plate as underplate, a saucer and a cup. All three are served at the one time.

Cover: Lay a dessert spoon instead of a soup spoon for clear soup.

- Serve the soup from the tureen into the cup with a silver soup ladle
- Place the complete set from the left

Petite marmite
This strong, French broth, garnished with cubes of beef, chicken winglets or chicken pieces and vegetables, is customarily served in lidded, earthenware individual pots (marmites). Sippets and grated cheese are offered.

Soup accompaniments

Beetroot juice, sour cream	Offered with Bortsch (a Russian or Polish soup made from duck)
Crôutons (sippets) Croûtes (flutes) Fromage râpé (grated cheese)	Sprinkled over soup; served separately from a sauceboat using a small ladle or spoon
Lemon wedge	Served on left side of underplate with certain clear soups
Paillettes (cheese straws)	Served on bread plate
Brown bread and butter, a quarter of lemon (usually also a glass of sherry or Madeira)	Offered with clear turtle soup (tortue clair)

Pastas (pâtés, pastes)

Macaroni, spaghetti, noodles (nouilles) and other pastes are served on an entrée plate.

Cover: a joint fork placed on the right hand side of the cover; a dessert spoon (or even table spoon if not too large) is also usually placed on the left.

Accompaniment: grated Parmesan cheese is offered with many pasta dishes.

Egg dishes

Oeuf sur le plat

Cover: small spoon, knife and fork.

Oeuf en cocotte

Cover: small spoon (teaspoon) served on underplate with cocotte dish.

Omelets

For omelets a fork alone is traditionally placed on the right hand side; but some establishments set a knife and fork.

When serving from a silver flat, first remove the extreme tips of the omelet with a spoon. Omelet may be served with spoon only.

Fish (poisson)

Cover: fish knife and fork, fish or entrée plate.

Sauced fish

Fish masked with a sauce (such as Mornay, Dugleré or Bonne Femme) require no preparation before serving, but:

- take care not to break the fish
- give each person a complete portion with adequate sauce and a helping of the steamed or boiled potato usually served

Unsauced fish cuts

A whole fish such as a Dover sole is usually grilled or meunière.

- Trim away the small bones around the fish
- Lift each fillet separately from the spine bone with a spoon and fork

For whole sole cooked in other styles, only trim off the small bones. Leave in the centre bone as it is nearly impossible to remove without breaking the fish.

Deep fried whole sole

When sole is deep fried, small bones are removed before cooking. Then as waiter:

- remove the fillets two at a time

- take out the centre bone
- re-build the fish onto the dish before serving

(See also Chapter 15 for treatment of sole.)

General guidance

As a rule:

- salt water fish are served without the head
- fresh water fish are served with the head still on
- fish preparation before serving must be done at the service table, or in the case of special dishes, such as 'truite au bleu', on a guéridon in front of the customer; but never on the customer's table
- if a fish portion is too large, divide it across the middle

Fish accompaniments

Deep fried (egg and breadcrumb) (frit à l'anglaise)	Tartare sauce, half lemon
Deep fried (in batter) (frit à l'Orly)	Tomato sauce (hot or cold), lemon
Grilled (grillé)	Tartare or Hollandaise (or derivative), Maître d'Hôtel (or anchovy or similar) butter
Poached (poché)	Hollandaise sauce, melted butter or egg sauce
Poached fresh salmon (saumon poché)	Cucumber salad (salade de concombre)
Cold salmon (saumon froid)	Lettuce, tomato, hard-boiled egg, cucumber salad, mayonnaise
Whitebait (blanchaille)	Cut brown bread and butter, lemon, cayenne pepper

Parsley with fish

Fresh parsley sprigs garnishing fish are intended to give colour; do not serve unless requested by the guest.
Fried parsley is part of the dish and should be served.

Cold lobster (homard froid)

Cover: fish knife and fork, lobster pick.

Half a lobster (the usual portion) is dressed in the shell on a silver flat on a bed of shredded lettuce. The usual garnish consists of half a hard-boiled egg, tomatoes and slices of cucumber.

First present the dish to the guest, then bring back to the service table for preparing.

- Place a little shredded lettuce on the guest's plate
- Using a spoon and fork, lift the flesh from the tail and cut away the shell part of the tail, leaving the flesh attached to the body of the fish
- Place this portion on top of the lettuce on the plate
- Using a clean napkin pick up the claw in your left hand
- Break the shell of the claw in half (this is cracked previously in the larder) and ease the flesh with the fork out of the shell
- Place this too on the plate
- Decorate the plate with the half hard-boiled egg, tomato and cucumber
- Having prepared all the plates in this way (when more than one person is being served), place them in front of each guest

Accompaniments: Mayonnaise sauce offered separately in a sauceboat. In addition, an oil and vinegar cruet can be placed on the table for this dish.

Main course and entrée

Cover: a joint knife and fork (and an entrée plate); but see variations below.

Service gear: a spoon and fork.

An entrée is complete in itself and is served on one silver dish, usually flat.

Main course service

No waiter preparation is usually required except for special à la carte dishes such as entrecôte, double Porterhouse steak, Châteaubriand, pheasant, grouse, etc.

First serve the meat, then pass vegetables and finally sauce from the sauceboat. In serving:

- give each person an equal portion
- ensure that garnish (vegetables, potatoes, watercress) is served to each guest
- French and English mustard are often required; pass them, do not just leave them on the table

Main course accompaniments

Meats

Roast lamb (agneau rôti)	Mint sauce (sauce menthe) or jelly
Roast saddle of mutton (selle de mouton rôtie)	Red currant jelly or onion sauce
Roast leg of mutton (gigot de mouton roti)	Red currant jelly or onion sauce

Roast shoulder of mutton (épaule de mouton rôtie)	Red currant jelly or onion sauce
Boiled leg of mutton (gigot de mouton bouilli)	Caper sauce (and purée of turnip)
Jugged hare (civet de lièvre)	Red currant jelly
Salmis of game (salmis de gibier)	Red currant jelly.
Roast beef (boeuf rôti)	Horseradish sauce, Yorkshire pudding
Boiled salt beef (silverside) (gite à la noix)	Carrots, onions, dumplings
Boiled fresh beef (French style) (boeuf bouilli à la française)	Grain or rock salt, gherkins, grated horseradish
Braised ham (jambon braisé)	Spinach (épinard), Madeira sauce (sauce Madère) or peach sauce
Grilled ham (jambon grillé) or boiled, baked ham	Appropriate sauce on menu such as mustard, tomato, horseradish
Braised tongue (langue de boeuf braisée)	Florentine garnish, spinach, Madeira sauce
Roast pork (porc rôti)	Sage and onion stuffing, apple sauce (demi-glace)
Roast veal (veau rôti)	Savoury herb stuffing, bacon and brown sauce (jus lié)
Curries (kari)	Boiled rice, chutney, poppadums, Bombay duck (Indian restaurants serve many other accompaniments)
Calf's head (tête de veau) (hot)	Vinaigrette or Gribiche sauce (some of the brains may be mixed in the sauce before serving)
Grills	Mustards (to be passed). Proprietory sauces (on table)
Cold meats (English buffet) (assiette Anglaise)	Mustards, pickles, chutney, proprietory sauces, relishes

Note: with beef, pork, ham, tongue, liver and kidneys, offer French and English mustard.

Poultry and game

Roast duck (caneton rôti)	Sage and onion stuffing (farce aux oignons), apple sauce (sauce pommes), roast gravy (jus)
Roast goose (oie rôti)	Sage and onion stuffing, apple sauce, roast gravy (jus)
Roast chicken (poulet rôti)	Bread sauce, roast gravy (possibly also bacon and sausage)

Roast turkey (dindon rôti)	Cranberry sauce, savoury herb or chestnut stuffing, chestnuts, chipolatas

Roast game

Grouse	
Partridge (perdreau, perdrix)	Bread sauce, fried breadcrumbs,
Pheasant (faisan)	roast gravy (jus)

Other game birds

Note: game chips usually accompany all roast birds.

Cover and service variations

Curry

Cover: knife, fork, dessert spoon.

Accompaniments: rice (often served as a ring, with the curry inside), poppadums, Bombay duck, chutneys.

Irish stew

Cover: meat knife and fork and soup spoon. Served into a soup plate with an underplate.

Accompaniment: Worcestershire sauce offered.

Lancashire hotpot

Cover and service: as for Irish stew.

Accompaniment: pickled red cabbage, offer Worcestershire sauce.

Hungarian goulash

Cover and service: as for Irish stew.

Accompaniment: noodles, pasta.

Main course clearing

When clearing, if no vegetable course follows and a sweet is next on the menu:

• remove side plates
• clear cruets, sauce bottles and other condiments as well as toast Melba and butter

- when all except glasses is clear, crumb down the table using a folded napkin and a plate
- place or bring down the sweet spoons and forks (which ever is house custom)
- place the sweet plates

Vegetables

Vegetables, particularly the finer ones, may be served as a separate course after the main one or, quite commonly today, as an introductory course.

Fresh asparagus and fresh globe artichoke (served as a separate course)

Cover: small (side) knife and dessert fork; finger bowl on table; hors d'oeuvre or fish-size plate (Figure 32).

Figure 32   A cover for asparagus or globe artichokes.

Vegetable accompaniments

Artichoke (artichaut), globe (hot)	Hollandaise, melted butter
Artichoke, globe (cold)	Mayonnaise, vinaigrette or Gribiche
Asparagus (asperge) (hot)	Hollandaise sauce, melted butter
Asparagus (cold)	Mayonnaise sauce, vinaigrette or Gribiche
Beets (betterave) (cold)	Vinaigrette
Broccoli (brocoli)	Hollandaise sauce
Cauliflower (choufleur)	Hollandaise, melted butter
Corn on the cob (mais)	Melted butter
Spinach (épinard) (en branches)	Cream, sometimes veal gravy

Salads

Salad, as an important component of a meal, should be more than a few lettuce leaves garnished with slivers of tomato, cucumber and beetroot. Salads give scope for waiters' flair in service.
Main types include:

Leaf salad Lettuce leaves, round (i.e. iceberg, cabbage lettuce) or cos, corn salad, chicory, endive, watercress, mixed as a 'composite' salad or individually as separate salads.

Heart salad Good quality round or cos lettuce with a tight heart, served in halves or quarters according to size.

Both types are served with cold meats and can be served with game or a grill on request.

Raw vegetable salad Shredded turnips, carrots, cabbage, celery, chicory, celeriac, spring onions, kohl-rabi, etc.

Cold cooked vegetables Chiefly root (whole or sliced) arranged decoratively. Carrots, turnips, onions, kohl-rabi, celery, celeriac, etc.

With fruit Chiefly used with game, or highly spiced or marinated dishes. Clean fruit flavour 'cuts' the richness of the dish.

Ingredients may be combined in any mixed salad according to customer's wish and season.

Service of salads

Covers: cut salads − a small fork on the plate.
heart salads − a small knife and fork.
certain fruit salads (e.g. those served in an orange or apple) − a teaspoon.

Place salads on the table at top left (10 to 12 o'clock) immediately before the rest of the course. The salad crescent (half moon or kidney plate) should fit the meat plate just above the side plate. The salads should all look uniform in size, design and position. To find room for the last salad, move the cruet or an odd glass or remove such items as ashtrays, menus, table numbers, water jugs.

Dressing salads

In high-class service, you may as waiter prepare dressings 'in the room'. Dressings are best blended with leaf salads in the bowl.

- Transfer the dressed salad to the salad plates, usually crescent shaped
- Place these with a dessert fork by the top left hand side of the guest's meat plate

If a customer asks to make his own dressing, adopt the following procedure.

- Place the salad bowl on the table above the cover
- Place the required ingredients at the top left
- Set a large plate with a large spoon and small fork in front of the customer
- When the guest has dressed the salad, you may remove it and arrange it on the salad plates

Some English customers may prefer salad oils other than olive oil, for example corn oil; others may appreciate sweetness. Hence, balance dressings according to customers' palates.

Dressing procedure

At the appropriate time, present the salad and ask if customers would like it dressed and, if so, whether they have a particular taste preference. Never dress salads, especially green salads, until the last moment or crispness will be lost. On receiving sanction for dressing, proceed as follows.

- Take a dinner or soup plate
- Measure onto it the salt, pepper, mustard and vinegar; mix
- Only if required, add other ingredients such as sugar or flavourings
- Add the oil
- Move the plate briskly back and forth with the left hand and whisk with a flat fork on the plate with the right, until a creamy texture is obtained
- Never mix dressings in a silver sauceboat or dish; the article will be badly scratched and ruined

Leaf salad

- First remove any garnish (egg, etc.) onto a plate
- Pour the dressing over the salad in the bowl
- With a spoon and fork lightly turn and twist the leaves in the bowl to impart a thin coating of dressing all over the leaves
- Place the dressed leaves neatly on salad plates
- Decorate with the garnish, which is then also dressed

Heart salad

- Do not flood the salad with dressing, but lightly mask the open part with dressing, using a teaspoon, so that the dressing sinks between the leaves
- Dress the garnish and arrange all onto the plate

Fruit-type salad

Acidulated cream dressing is usually employed. Many such salads are already dressed. If they also contain green salad, they need dressing at table.

- Arrange these salads on plates
- Lightly mask only the fruit with the dressing

Dressings (see Table 10)

Popular dressings include:

French: Salt, pepper (mill), French mustard and one part vinegar to three parts oil

English: Salt, pepper, English mustard and two parts vinegar to one part oil, with caster sugar to taste.

American: Similar to English with equal oil and vinegar

Mayonnaise: Mayonnaise sauce thinned with vinegar and lemon juice to a dressing consistency

Lemon: Salt, pepper, fresh lemon juice and olive oil to taste (with caster sugar as may be required)

Sauce vinaigrette: Salt, pepper, one part vinegar to two parts olive oil. (Also used for certain hot dishes, as with plain boiled calf's head.). French or English mustard may be added to the guest's requirements

Sauce Ravigotte: Vinaigrette with a heavy garnish of chopped chives, chervil, tarragon, capers and parsley

Sauce Gribiche: Mayonnaise dressing garnished with chopped gherkins, capers, chervil, tarragon, parsley and strips of hard egg white

Acidulated cream: Fresh cream and fresh lemon juice seasoned with salt. Other items are added according to salad. (Used mainly for the fruit-type salads)

Thousand island: Mayonnaise dressing with a little chili sauce and chopped red pimento, chives and green peppers

Table 10   Some salads with suggested dressings.

Name	Ingredients	Dressing
Archiduc	Julienne of beetroot, endives, truffle and potato	Vinaigrette
Augustin	Heart of cos lettuce with French beans, quartered tomato and hard-boiled egg, green peas	Mayonnaise
Demi-deuil	Heart of lettuce with strips of truffle and potato	Vinaigrette
Eleanora	Heart of cos lettuce garnished with base of artichoke and asparagus points	Mayonnaise
Eve	Scooped out apple filled with dice of apple, pineapple and banana	Acidulated cream
Florida	Hearts of lettuce with quartered oranges	Acidulated cream

Française	Lettuce leaves with quartered tomato and hard-boiled egg, sliced beetroot and cucumber	French
Gauloise	Leaves of cos lettuce with strips of fresh nuts	Mayonnaise
Legumes (de)	Diced potato with chopped French beans, green peas and cauliflower	Vinaigrette
Louisette	Heart of cos lettuce with quarters of tomato and skinned, de-pipped grapes	Vinaigrette
Lorette	Corn salad with strips of beetroot and celery root	Vinaigrette
Niçoise	French beans, quartered tomato, sliced potato, decorated with fillets of anchovy, olives and capers	Vinaigrette
Rachel	Strips of celery and truffle, base of artichoke, potato and asparagus points	Mayonnaise

Sweet course

Cover: dessert spoon and fork (moved down from the top of the place setting to the right and left side).

Lunch-time cold sweets

These are usually presented on a trolley, with service similar to that from hors d'oeuvre trolleys. Cut and serve gâteaux and flans with a cake slice; use a serving spoon and fork for other items.

- Wheel the trolley round the table
- Serve each guest individually according to his instructions

Hot sweets

- Place hot plates before guests
- Hold the serving dish on your left hand
- Serve with a spoon and fork or a spoon only, according to the type of sweet

En coupe service

For sweets served in 'coupe' (in silver or glass cups):

- place the coupe on a sweet plate with a teaspoon alongside it on the plate

For ice cream, pass wafers separately (arranged neatly on a doyley-covered silver flat or plate); never stick wafers in the ice-cream.

If a customer, after taking a trolley sweet additionally orders at the same time another sweet which is served in a coupe, then spoon the sweet from the coupe to serve by the side of the other sweet on the same plate.

Cheese and biscuits

Cover: place clean side plate and side knife in front of each guest.

On the table: set in the middle a fresh dish of butter (on an underplate with a fork alongside) with also a doyley-covered dish or plate containing a selection of biscuits such as cream crackers (whole tins are sometimes passed either wrapped in a napkin or in a silver container) and celery in a glass (watercress may also be offered).

The cheeseboard is normally brought to the guests' table on a trolley or placed on an adjacent side-table. Be sure you can identify each cheese featured (Figure 33).

Service: present the cheeseboard to each customer.

- Cut a piece of selected cheese with a special knife. Remove any rind or wrappers
- Place the cheese portion on the customer's plate
- Once the cheese has been portioned, replace the knife with a clean one

Cream cheese: caster sugar, cream (or sour cream) and sweet biscuits may be requested.

Savouries

Cover: a joint knife and fork. A hot plate put in front of each guest.

On the table: place a plate covered with a folded napkin carrying salt and pepper mill, red pepper and Worcestershire sauce. Add other sauces according to the nature of savoury.

Service: in some cases pass French and English mustard.

Figure 33 A selection of cheeses.

Fresh fruit

Cover: half fill a finger bowl with tepid water on a fruit plate, a fruit fork to the left and a fruit knife to the right also on the same plate (rest the tip of the knife on the prongs of the fork).

From the customer's left, place this whole cover in front of the guest.

- Lift the finger bowl and place it above the plate
- Again from the left, present the fruit basket, with which is a bowl of cold water, to the customer
- Place this bowl of water on the table while serving the customer
- Carry the basket on your left hand
- In your right hand hold a pair of scissors

Apple, orange or pear

- The customer helps himself from the basket

Grapes

- Cut the stalk with your grape scissors, dip the grapes in a bowl of cold water

- Serve the small bunch of grapes onto the customer's plate with the help of the grape scissors
- Repeat for the next customer

Fresh Pineapple

- Remove from the basket onto a cold meat plate
- With a napkin, hold the pineapple on its side and slice off the top
- Cut a further slice before the portion to be served is cut
- Replace the top on the pineapple, return it to the basket and clear the basket
- Insert a table fork into the core of the slice, insert the point of a sharp knife and cut around the fruit between the skin and the flesh to remove the skin, turning the fork to revolve the slice and aid the skin's removal
- Keeping the fork in the core, cut with the point of the knife between the flesh and core to extract the core on the fork

Now serve the ring of fresh pineapple as it is; alternatively cut it into segments, place in a bowl, add caster sugar and a measure of kirsch, mix and then serve.

15
Guéridon Work and Carving

For some dishes mentioned in Chapter 14 special service tools or equipment may be used. This may also include preparation by the waiter at the sideboard (guéridon) or trolley.

Guéridon basics

The principles of guéridon (side-table) usage were referred to in Chapters 11 and 12 and you will have noted that the guéridon is used to a greater or lesser extent in silver service generally. The term guéridon service, however, generally indicates soignée (careful and polished) service in up-market operations and especially when portioning, carving, salad mixing or serving flambé food.

For preparations such as filleting of cooked fish (particularly Dover soles), carving poultry and game, and finishing dishes such as pancakes, work is performed on a small service table or trolley with a réchaud (hot plate) or spirit lamp (for cooking) in front of the customer.

Always deal with the dish in full view of the guest; for after presentation the dish should not leave the customer's sight. Thus, do not transfer anything to the sideboard and deal with it with your back to the guest, obscuring the service.

Where no guéridons are provided, portioning must, of course, be done at the waiter's sideboard; but still try to work in view of your guest.

These advanced techniques are more comprehensively covered in a restaurateur's guide to *Guéridon and Lamp Cookery* (John Fuller, published by Hutchinson, 1979) which includes carving, salad mixing, speciality dishes as well as flambage. This chapter is, therefore, confined to selected examples which illustrate some of the fundamentals in working from the guéridon.

Selective guéridon usage

A more selective use of special dishes and special services accompanies the trend for shorter menus whether table d'hôte or modified à la carte. Many waiters and waitresses, though not expected to have mastered the entire range of service skills, may be required to serve a more limited range of establishment specialities. One or two such items may involve guéridon presentation. Examples of guéridon or special services featured in restaurants or steak houses with a limited menu at a popular price include side-table preparations of salad dressing and tossed salad; baked jacket potato (pomme au four) with butter or cream finish.

Special services, not necessarily from the guéridon, may include dishes such as asparagus, because an establishment may wish to exploit equipment like drainer dishes and tongs. Smoked salmon may even be regarded as a special service, in transferring slivers from the silver flat to the guest's plate and the presentation of its accompaniments.

Thus, special dishes and services need not be confined to top-level waiters in large, luxury establishments as part of an all embracing repertoire; for some may be featured selectively (possibly with establishment adaptations and variations in certain cases) in restaurants of different and more modest type.

Special equipment

Many implements, gadgets and types of dish have been evolved for serving different foods. They tend to be applied to more costly items or to those which present difficulties in serving or eating. The factors behind special restaurant equipment and service are:

- to facilitate waiters serving or guests eating, or
- to enhance service to aid merchandizing a dish

These two factors cannot always both be reconciled. It is impracticable to have too much special equipment, involving an extensive and elaborate inventory. Because of the labour involved in inventory checking, and for cost and efficiency reasons, it is desirable to keep service equipment stocked on the sideboard at its simplest.

Once a waiter has learned the knack of manipulating a service spoon and fork then these two simple items can when splayed lift large, flat objects (obviating the need for slice) and hold long, thin objects (rendering tongs unnecessary).

This is why many other gadgets have either never 'caught on' or eventually fall into disuse. Asparagus tongs are nowadays seldom encountered. An asparagus rack and underplate are used much less than a simple, oval flat covered with a napkin.

It is not always easy, therefore, to decide when it is justifiable to use special tools in waiting or to provide them for the guest at table. Moreover, staff skills must always be taken into account. Only where merchandizing will be substantially enhanced is there a clear case for a special piece of equipment or technique. Thus, do not assume that traditional tools and techniques are always justified.

Lamps (réchauds)

Spirit lamps have been largely replaced by gas lamps which are easier to maintain and control.

Each day before service, lamps must be thoroughly checked to ensure:

- cleanliness
- replacement gas cylinders are available (or that they are charged with methylated spirit if appropriate)
- wicks on spirit models are adequate for the forthcoming service period

Carving

Carving in the restaurant itself (as distinct from 'behind the scenes' in the kitchen) may be done by a specialist carver (trancheur) from buffets or trolleys or by a chef sent in from the kitchen. In up-market restaurants many items are carved by the waiter on a guéridon or side-table in front of the guest.

Mise en place

A chef trancheur uses long, thin-bladed French- or English-style carving knives and a double-tined carving fork; but waiters at the guéridon rely chiefly on an ordinary table knife and fork or fish knife and fork as appropriate.

Otherwise, buffet or trolley mise en place could include the following.

A thin carving knife (tranchelard) about 32 cm (13 inches) long for joints such as ham, roast sirloin of beef and also smoked salmon.
A shorter, broader knife about 24 cm (9 inches) long for saddles of veal or lamb.
A smaller, strong-bladed knife, about 18 cm (7 inches) long, for game and double steaks such as Châteaubriand and double entrecôte.
A carving board with a groove for meat juice (the board may be pre-heated on an electric hotplate).
A lamp and chafing dish in case a guest wishes a less rare portion.

Tools and techniques

Although a waiter normally works with ordinary service cutlery, he probably reserves a well-sharpened table knife for carving meat items like double steaks. Blunt knives cause: heavy pressure and the squeezing out of too much juice; misshapen slices; danger of meat sliding off plate should the knife slip; and other accidents.

Whoever does the carving, the aim is to keep the item as near as possible to its original arrangement and for portions (and what remains) to be properly dressed. Speed (without undue haste), skill and economy are essential in achieving carving objectives.

Carving needs preparation and practice. Keep knives sharp, for pressure when carving should be light; otherwise slices and their surface will be uneven. (Sharpen knives outside the restaurant itself.) Always carve against the grain of the meat (except for saddles of lamb or mutton where one method cuts at right angles to the rib bone). It is important to learn the bone structure of all items to be carved.

Rules of slicing

Smoked salmon : very finely
Boiled ham and roast beef : thinly
Lamb, mutton and pork : a little more thickly

Treatment in the room

At table

Items commonly carved by waiters include:

fish	–	sole, smoked salmon
poultry	–	especially chicken
beef	–	double steaks (e.g. Porterhouse, T-bone, double entrecôte or sirloin, Châteaubriand and rib steak)
lamb	–	best-end (carré d'agneau)

From buffets

Waiters may carve other hot or cold items including:

fish	–	whole salmon, salmon trout, turbot and other fish
poultry	–	especially turkey
joints of meat	–	ham on the bone, ribs of beef, saddles of lamb, legs of pork and lamb for example

This chapter does not seek to deal exhaustively with carving (especially items dealt with by chefs from buffets and trolleys). The examples which follow serve, however, to indicate basic procedures of the waiter at the side-table.

Fish

For smaller fish: use ordinary fish knife and fork.
For larger fish: use fish slices or fish carvers.
Never use ordinary steel knives; they convey an unpleasant taste to fish.

Whole salmon

- Remove the skin from the upper side
- run your knife from top to tail to detach the upper fish from the bone
- carve obliquely into slices (about two inches)

Sole (grilled, fried or meunière)

Mise en place: large warmed plate, two table forks (or tablespoon and fork).
(Some prefer to use two forks, others spoon and fork; but there is general
agreement that a knife should never be used in boning a sole).

Method

- With two table forks, transfer the fish from its silver flat to the warm plate
- Remove head and tail
- If they have not been trimmed away prior to cooking, remove the fringe
  of small fin bones (the sidebones sometimes called the wing or feather
  bones) by pressing round the edge of the sole with the edge of a fork
- Press the prongs of your two forks down through each side of the
  backbone
- Ease the top and bottom fillets together as one piece from the backbone
- Continue to ease from head to tail until the bone is clear of fillet
- Lift away bone
- Re-form the fillets into the shape of the sole and lift it back onto the silver

Fish cutlets and tronçons

Round, white fish such as cod, halibut, and haddock are often cut, including
the bone, into steaks, cutlets or tronçons. When grilled or meunière proceed
as follow:

Mise en place: large warm plate, table spoon and fork (and/or fish knife and
fork)

Method

- Steady the fish by the flat of a spoon, remove skin by securing one end
  with a fork
- Twist the fork so that the skin curls round the fork and removes it from
  around the cutlet (normally it comes away cleanly, but may be eased as
  necessary by the spoon held in the other hand) (*Note*: some waiters use
  a fish knife and fork for skinning)
- Once the skin is away, remove the centre bone

Turbot

- With a fish knife cut down the centre from head to tail
- Make further cuts at 5 cm intervals at right angles from this central line
- When the top is completed, remove the bone
- Remove the black skin from the underside and treat similarly

Poultry

Roast chicken

Mise en place: sharpened table knife, table fork, large, warmed plate, lamp (réchaud)

Method (Figure 34)
First stage
- With a fork inside lift the bird from the silver
- Tilt the chicken (still suspended over the silver flat) to drain its juice into the accompanying sauceboat of gravy
General
- Sever through bones only at connecting joints; never attempt to chop through
- As portions are removed from the chicken, either
  (a) transfer to the silver flat for passing to guests, or
  (b) portion directly onto guests' plates

Second stage

- Outline with the knife tip on the upright chicken the cut for later removal of wings
- Turn the bird onto its side, holding securely, with your fork inserted into the leg at its joint
- Insert the knife between thigh and body, and cut around, finally severing at the connecting joint and remove the leg (gentle pulling on the fork should easily detach)
- Cut in two through the joint and replace the leg on the silver dish
- Slice off the wing severing at the pinion joint and also transfer to the silver
- Turn the bird over and similarly remove the other leg and wing, arranging them on the silver
- With the bird on its breast, remove the wishbone section and add to the portions on the silver flat. (The breast may optionally, if large, be cut in two)
- Serve when carving is completed

Roast duck

- Remove legs and wings as for a chicken

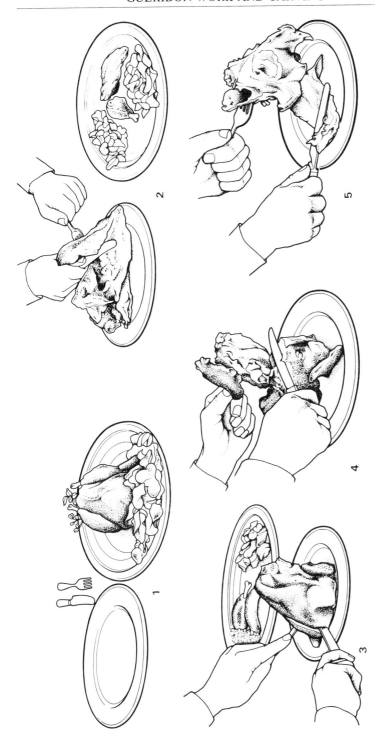

Figure 34 Carving a chicken. (1) Mise en place: hot dinner plate, table knife and fork and the platter of chicken (after presentation to the guest). (2) With one leg removed, divided into two and replaced on the platter, the second leg is removed. Note the knife dividing the meat at the joint. (3) With both legs removed, sever through a portion of the breast to remove the wing by severing at the wing bone joint. (4) Completion of the wing joint severance with the chicken on its side. (5) Removing the final white breast meat, showing the carcase remaining.

- Carve the carcase breast in several slices
- If stuffed, scoop out and serve the stuffing with a spoon

Guinea fowl

Carve as chicken.

Turkey or goose

- Detach the legs without removing them from the dish
- Cut thin slices from the side of the breast and slices from the thigh
- If stuffed, serve a spoonful

Game birds

Grouse ⎫
Partridge ⎬ Split in two through the breast bone
Pigeon ⎭
Pheasant: carve into thin slices
Quail: serve whole
Snipe ⎫
Woodcock ⎬ Divide into two

Wild duck à la presse (sauvage à la presse)

Mise en place: a press, silver frying pan, silver flat, salt, pepper mill, half lemon, chafing lamp, serving spoon and fork and sharp knife, port wine, brandy, conical strainer, silver sauceboat, wild duck par-cooked from the kitchen.

Method

- Put into the frying pan a few crushed peppercorns, a strip of lemon zest and a glass of port
- Over the lamp reduce by half
- Having removed the skin, carve the breast of the wild duck into thin slices
- Put these on one side (on silver flat)
- Cut away and discard any fatty parts of the carcase, remove the legs and chop them up with the carcase
- Press the chopped parts well in the press catching the blood in the sauceboat
- Chop up the duck's liver and place in the frying pan with the gravy, a pat of butter, salt and pepper, lemon juice and the blood
- Cook for a few minutes
- Pour brandy over, flame and then pour through a conical strainer over the sliced duck
- Re-heat over the lamp and serve
- Serve orange salad on a separate plate

Meat small cuts

Double steaks to serve two are normally carved by the waiter. As for chicken, do not carve these and other meat cuts on their silver (or other metal) service platter, but on a warm dinner plate. (Use a carving board for larger joints.)

Châteaubriand (double fillet steak, grilled or sauté au beurre)

Typical is the Châteaubriand, a double-size steak for two persons cut from the head of the fillet (the thickest end which passes through the sirloin into the rump). It arrives in the restaurant if grilled (though it may be sauté au beurre) with a portion of grilled suet and is often served with maître d'hôtel butter or sauce Béarnaise.

Mise en place: sharpened table knife, fork, two large warmed plates, lamp (réchaud).

Method

- Transfer the steak to the plate
- Secure the meat with the back of the fork without piercing it
- Trim as necessary with the knife and fork; but note that the charred exterior is esteemed by most guests
- Holding the knife at a slight angle, cut slantwise about four slices (about 2 cm (¾ inch)), transferring them back onto the silver flat (on réchaud or hot plate)
- Similarly slice the suet and place appropriate pieces on the silver
- Cut the remaining suet into small pieces and with any steak trimmings, squeeze these suet pieces between the two plates
- Pour the resultant juice* over the carved steak
- Serve onto the warm plates, adding any accompanying butter or sauce

Côte à l'Os (rib steak, grilled)

Usually for two, however a larger côte de boeuf steak may be sufficient for four portions. Hold with a napkin the trimmed end of the bone and remove the meat in one piece from the bone. Carve the meat obliquely from right to left into slices as for Châteaubriand above, and immediately serve on well-warmed plates together with any garnish.

Entrecôte double (double strip sirloin steak)

Cut off the fatty end tip; then carve obliquely as for Châteaubriand (Figure 35). Replace the slices on the service dish, add the juice from the steak (the trimmings may be squeezed between two plates to add to the juices).

---

*To this juice may be added further jus rôti, mustard and/or Worcestershire sauce and/or sherry and seasoning for blending in a chafing dish to form a sauce.

Figure 35   Carving double entrecôte (double strip sirloin steak).

T-bone and Porterhouse steak

These steaks from the unboned sirloin include the fillet and contrefilet meat. The Porterhouse is cut from the rump end of the sirloin, that is where the fillet is thickest.

Cut away the meat from both sides of the the bone. Then carve both pieces obliquely as before, cutting the fillet into slightly thinner slices. Give each guest an equal number of slices from both.

Lamb

Best end (carré d'agneau)

To avoid piercing the meat, secure the joint with the back of the fork; alternatively insert the fork close to the bone. Using the rib bones to guide your knife, remove cutlets either one by one or in twos, that is, including two cutlets to form a portion (Figure 36).

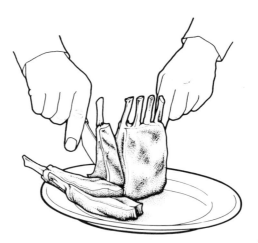

Figure 36   Carving best end of lamb (carré d'agneau).

Soufflés

Sweet soufflés include: chocolate, Grand-Marnier, Kirsch.

Savoury soufflés include: cheese (au fromage), spinach (aux épinards)

Soufflés incorporate stiffly beaten whites of eggs and are cooked to order; for unless served immediately they may collapse.

Time your order in liaison with the kitchen so that you can serve the soufflé when it is ready without customers having to wait.

Allow 20 minutes, so alert the pâtissier just before you serve the preceding course.

Sweet items

Omelet soufflé Surprise or Baked Alaska

Covers: dessert spoon and fork.

Service: on to cold dessert plates.

For these ice cream items with a hot outside, egg yolk, sugar and stiffly beaten white of egg are mixed and piped decoratively onto thick layers of ice cream, which are already on a thick layer of syrup-soaked sponge centred on a large silver flat. Browned rapidly in a very hot oven just before it is to be served, the ice cream remains unmelted.

Variants include:

omelet Vesuvius (incorporating a small timbale of flaming spirit)
omelet soufflé en surprise jubilee (alternative title grand succés) with a timbale of cherries jubilee (see below).

Cherries jubilee (cérises jubilee)

Large stoned cherries poached in syrup are placed in a silver timbale or bowl or in individual small silver timbales with handles. Kirsch is poured over them, ignited and served flaming. They are also often served with vanilla ice or a simple biscuit glacé.

Flambé sweets

Crêpe Suzette

Mise en place (four persons): one orange, eight cubes of sugar, caster sugar sifter, 60 g butter, one measure of Curaçao, one measure of brandy, eight pancakes (from the kitchen). The crêpe Suzette unit is illustrated in Figure 37.

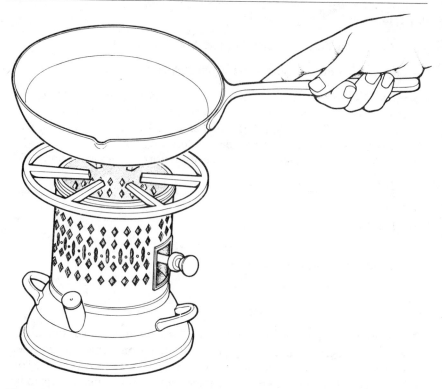

Figure 37   Crêpe Suzette unit.

Method: Suzette sauce

- Rub the cubes of sugar on the rind of one orange until they have thoroughly absorbed the colour
- Place the sugar into the sauceboat with the squeezed juice from the orange and juice of half a lemon
- Add the curaçao and the softened butter, mixing all together into an emulsion

Stage two

- Put a little caster sugar into the frying pan over the lamp
- When the sugar becomes sticky, add one or two spoons of sauce Suzette and continue to cook until it thickens and caramelizes
- Using a fork, roll up one pancake and place in this caramel for about half a minute
- Turn it over and then neatly fold in four with the fork and push to one side of the pan
- Add a little more sauce and sugar to the frying pan and similarly dress another pancake

- Continue until all the pancakes are folded in four, lying in the pan
- Sprinkle over a little sugar, pour in the brandy and allow to catch alight
- Serve, with a spoon and fork, the flaming pancakes on to hot sweet plates ready placed in front of the guests

Flamed peaches (pêches flambées)

Mise en place: four fresh peaches, sugar syrup, caster sugar sifter, one measure of kirsch.

Method

- Peel fresh peaches
- Poach in syrup flavoured with kirsch, in a silver timbale; take out when soft
- Put in a silver frying pan with sugar sprinkled over them
- Mask them with kirsch and allow to catch alight
- Serve while lighted, with a spoon and fork, on to the hot plates ready placed in front of the customers

16

Breakfasts and Floor Service

Breakfast and beverages service are important in impressing guests, yet may be overshadowed by the gastronomic interest of luncheons, dinners and banquets. For hotel guests, breakfast is often the last meal taken before departure. Its service gives them one of their final impressions of the establishment and its staff.

Waiters with an international clientele will soon realize that breakfasts differ widely. Scandinavians and the Dutch go beyond the basic continental breakfast and may include slices of cheese, boiled eggs, salami, cold ham, fruits, grated chocolate (Holland) and even pastries (in Finland and Spain) amongst breakfast choices. The Israel 'buffet' breakfast with salad items, smoked fish, etc. is now widely adapted in other countries. Do not regard any breakfast request as strange; British and American cooked breakfasts may seem just as strange to other nationals.

Hotel breakfasts

Two types of breakfast are served:

- plain or continental
- full British (or American) breakfast (including more substantial and cooked items)

Continental breakfast

Continental breakfast (Figure 38) consists of a beverage, usually coffee or tea, but possibly chocolate or milk, with a service of rolls (and possibly croissants and brioches) and butter with accompanying conserve (marmalade, jam). In Britain toast is also offered. This basic breakfast is often called by the French term café complet or thé complet. Today, fruit juice or, possibly, fresh fruit or fruit compote are often included or taken as extras.

British breakfast

As continental breakfasts have become more popular, the English (or American) breakfast (Figure 38) has become less extensive than it was pre-war. Formerly, choices were made from menus which offered fruit juices and fruits, porridge and other cereals, fish, egg dishes with bacon, sausages and offals together with the usual variety of breads, toasts, preserves and beverages. Today, only three courses are normally chosen:

- fruit juice, fruits or cereal
- a fish or egg and bacon type dish
- toast, rolls, etc. and preserves (jams, etc.)

Some set menu simplifications, for example 'Club Breakfast', may reduce this to a preliminary juice followed by bacon and eggs. This eases costs and speeds service.

Breakfast items

Though a breakfast menu will indicate a greater limit of choice, it may feature selections from the following.

Fresh fruits: grapefruit, melon, fresh fruit salad, apple, apricot, pear, peach, grapes, etc. (fruits may also possibly be offered after the cooked course).

Compotes: figs, prunes, apples, mixed fruit.

Juices: orange, grapefruit, pineapple, tomato.

Cereals: Cornflakes, Grapenuts, Shredded Wheat, etc., porridge (also for American menus: cracked wheat, buckwheat, hominy grits and an extended selection of patent cereals).

Fish: grilled mackerel, kippers, herrings, bloaters, smoked Finnan haddock, Arbroath smokies, fish cakes, kedgeree. Fried or meunière: turbot, cod, plaice, whiting, sole, etc. (plainly served with simple sauces, if any).

Eggs: poached, boiled, coddled, fried, en cocotte, sur le plat, scrambled and omelets. Pancakes (especially for USA guests).

Accompaniments: sauté or fried potatotes, baked beans, potato fritters, potato cakes or scones, bubble and squeak, tomato, mushrooms, waffles.

Possible cold items: ham, tongue, pressed salt beef, with accompaniments of sauté potatoes, hashed potatoes, etc.

Preserves: jams, honey, syrup, marmalade.

Drinks: tea, coffee, chocolate and, possibly, 'patent' beverages.

Bread: rolls, croissants, toast, Melba toast, brioche.

Other breakfast or early meal items which may be noted include:

Brunch Supposedly a blend of breakfast and lunch dishes; usually a mixed

LIGHT BREAKFAST £5.75

Choice of:
Fruit Juices,
Grapefruit, Orange,
Pineapple, Tomato, V.8.

* * * * *

Rolls, Croissants, Toast, Ryvita
Griddle Cakes
with Butter
Marmalade, Jam or Honey.

* * * * *

Cereals
or
Half Fresh Grapefruit
or Boiled Eggs.

* * * * * *

Tea — China or Indian
Coffee, Coffee Hag or Chocolate.

Breakfast is served in the Restaurant
from 7.15 a.m. to 10 a.m. Monday to Saturday
and from 8 a.m. to 10 a.m. Sunday and Bank Holidays.

ENGLISH BREAKFAST £8.50

Choice of:
Stewed Fruit, Fresh **Fruit, Melon**,
Half Fresh **Grapefruit**
or
Cereals or **Porridge**
Selection of
Oak **Smoked Kipper**,
Finnan **Haddock** (20 mins.)
Grilled **Fillet of Plaice**
or
Eggs
Fried, Poached, Scrambled or
Boiled with Bacon,
Tomato, Sausage, Mushrooms
or
Roast Beef Hash
Sauté Potatoes
or Cold **York Ham**.

* * * * *

Rolls, Croissants, Toast, Ryvita
with Butter
Marmalade, Jam or Honey.

* * * * *

Tea — China or Indian
Coffee, Coffee Hag or Chocolate.

All prices include Service and Value Added Tax.

SPECIALITIES

Potted Smoked Salmon £2.75

* * * * *

Haddock Monte Carlo (15 mins.) £3.75
Kedgeree (15 mins.) £4.00

* * * * *

Minute Steak and Mushrooms £5.50
Devilled Kidneys £4.00
Black Pudding and Bacon £3.25

* * * * *

Scrambled Egg Wiltshire £3.25
Omelette — Tomato, Ham or Mushroom £3.00

* * * * *

Cold Roast Beef £4.50
Cold Ox Tongue £4.50

* * * * *

Griddle Cakes and Maple Syrup £1.25
Cinnamon Toast £1.00
Fresh Fruit Salad £2.50
Fresh Strawberries and Cream £2.75
Sliced Fresh Orange £2.75

* * * * *

This selection of dishes is offered as an addition to the
light breakfast menu.

* * * * *

Bucks Fizz £6.00

* * * * *

Mineral Water
Ashbourne £1.65 per bottle
Malvern £1.10 per bottle
Vichy £1.65 per bottle
Perrier £1.65 per bottle
San Pelegrino £1.65 per bottle

Figure 38 Example of full and continental breakfast menus, Brown's Hotel, Albermale Street, London W1.

grill (or more accurately griddle fry) featuring, egg, bacon, sausage, mushroom, tomato, French fried potatoes with possibly baked beans, spaghetti in tomato sauce or similar items.

Muesli: Often called Bircher Muesli (after Dr Bircher Benner who pioneered it as a health dish in Switzerland), a raw porridge-type dish of raw oats (sometimes milk-soaked), honey, chopped, raw apple (and bananas or other fruit), raisins or sultanas. Served usually in cereal plate with cream.

Breakfast mise en place

Full English breakfast requires more preparation in the dining room before service than any other meal.

- Grapefruit need to be cut and oranges squeezed (these tasks must never be done the previous night)
- Fruit juices, cereals, jugs of cream and cold milk must be arranged on a table (usually cold buffet table) in the dining room
- Services of jam, honey and marmalade need to be prepared
- Jugs of iced water with glasses should be available 'en place' on each sideboard
- Tables require much preparation as more items are set on them than at any other meal

Previous evening's preparation

To be ready on time for breakfast service, as much mise en place as possible is done the previous night.

- A clean tablecloth is laid on the table
- The cover is set

Full breakfast cover (Figure 39)

- To the right   — medium-sized plate, a joint knife (and possibly a fish knife*)
- To the left   — a joint fork (and possibly a fish fork*)
- In front   — a sweet fork, handle to the left and a sweet spoon, handle to the right
- On the left hand side of this, a side plate with a side knife on the right edge of the plate in line with the other cutlery
- A slop basin, a set of cruets and an ashtray placed symmetrically on the table

* Fish knife and fork are often omitted in present day lay-ups.

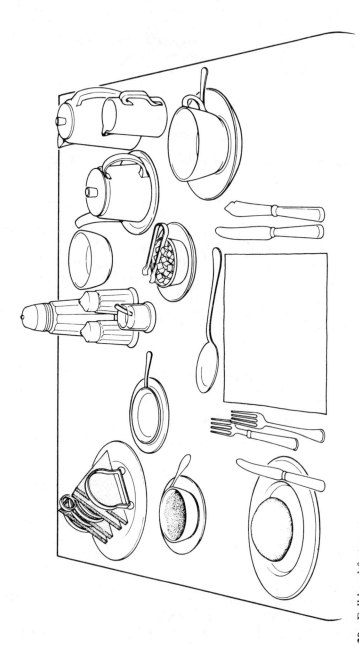

Figure 39 Full breakfast cover.

Continental breakfast cover

- Side plate, a small knife on its right
- Slop basin and ashtray positioned as in full breakfast cover

Morning covers completion

Next morning complete the table settings with:

- breakfast-sized cups and saucers (placed beside the tip of the fish knife), tea spoons
- table napkins (placed square on the medium-sized plate)
- a bowl of soft and a bowl of lump sugar placed on each table, together with a jug of cold milk, a jug of cream and a service of preserves (marmalade, honey and jam — often in miniature jars)

Flowers

Floral decorations are not generally used for breakfast but are most acceptable when provided.

Morning mise en place

During this same time, if there are commis, they:

- attend to sideboards, stacking up cutlery, plates, cups, saucers, napkins, large and small tablecloths and anything which may be required during service
- prepare grapefruits, orange juice, grapefruit juice, tomato juice, etc., and jugs of iced water
- assemble condiments to include fresh mustard, Worcestershire sauce, vinegar

If there are no commis, waiters attend to these tasks.

Never bring into the room nor keep on the sideboard anything which is not required for breakfast. Unnecessary items only hinder a waiter during service.

Taking orders

General instructions regarding handing of the menu, manner and checking apply. Preface your enquiry regarding guests' wishes with a request for the room number.

Breakfast menus are presented to each guest.

- Take the order in the usual manner (see Chapter 10)
- Write any instructions given by a customer regarding the preparation of his order (timing of egg, etc.) on the check

Breakfast service

Service is fundamentally the same as for any other meal. The commis (or the waiter himself where there are no commis) brings dishes from the various serveries to the sideboard. The waiter verifies the correctness of the order and then serves it. First-class breakfast service is done on silver, but many hotels adopt plate service to expedite service.

For plate service the waiter usually collects orders from the kitchen and his commis (if he has one) attends to still room requirements.

Serving beverages

For continental breakfast, serve the beverage immediately. At English breakfast, place the beverage on the table with the preliminary course, or after the preliminary course if this has been juice or fruit, and prior to serving the main course. Coffee may be 'pour 'n serve' otherwise guests serve themselves with beverages from pots. Thus, place the beverage service at the top right hand corner of the senior lady in the party, or according to the people present and the beverages required.

Place tea pot and hot water jug (or coffee pot and hot milk jug) on side plates or stands. Other beverages (chocolate, etc.) are similarly placed on the table in jugs for customers to serve themselves.

Breakfast sequence

Serve (or place on the table) coffee (or other beverage), toast, hot rolls, brioches and croissants at the same time as cereals (including porridge) unless a guest stipulates otherwise.

Breads and toast

Toast may be served either in a toast rack on underplate, or in a napkin (perhaps within a basket) The aim is to ensure crispness, as densely packed toast becomes soggy.

Bread rolls, croissants, and brioches are also often presented in a basket or napkin-lined silver basket. They are not normally repeatedly 'passed' but left in the basket or dish on the table for guests to help themselves.

Fruit, juices and cereal

Grapefruit, other fresh fruit, compotes, fruit and tomato juice, are also served (if not self-helped) at this stage and/or porridge or cereal.

Juices

Pour fruit juices into goblets or glasses from glass jugs at the sideboard or buffet and bring to the table on side plates, covered with a doyley in better-class operations.

In high-class service, the fruit container may be brought to the guest in an underbowl filled with crushed ice.

If serving *tomato juice*, offer the cruet and Worcestershire sauce and provide a teaspoon.

Grapefruit

Fresh halves of grapefruit are normally served in silver coupes on an underplate with sundae spoon (or similar spoon), but also may be served on crushed ice.

It may be the duty of waiting staff to prepare grapefruit for service.

- After halving, use a sharp-pointed small knife (couteau d'office) to remove the centre pith
- Carefully run the knife around each segment to detach the segments from skin and pith skeleton
- A canned cherry is often placed in the centre
- Place sugar sifter on the table.

Cereals and porridge

Cereals are often placed into dishes at the sideboard or buffet table for the customer to serve himself. Porridge is usually brought from the kitchen already in the dish and hot milk — and, desirably, cream (cold) — is served. Brown sugar is offered. (Service of porridge from a timbale or tureen at the table is unusual, even in luxury hotels, but is acceptable.

Service of main hot breakfast dishes

Next follows any main cooked item selected: fish (especially kippers, haddock), various combinations of eggs, bacon, sausages, tomatoes, black pudding, etc. Assume that all cooked items are ready or can be quickly prepared. Except in the highest-class hotels, these are more often than not pre-plated in the kitchen.

Timing orders is not usually a difficulty, though interpretation of requirements sometimes may be.

Times for eggs

Always ask guests about their preferences in the matter of cooking times, especially eggs. For boiled eggs, precise cooking times depend on the size. Large eggs as provided in good hotel service take:

hard boiled	— 8-10 minutes
soft boiled	— 5 minutes

lightly soft boiled $-$ $3\frac{1}{2}$ -5 minutes
coddled $-$ 6 minutes (1 minute in boiling water, 5 minutes
                 continued immersion in the water off boil)

Main course clearance

When you clear away the plate used for the main course:

- remove any spare (i.e. unused) silver left on the table
- remove the side plate to directly in front of the guest
- move the toast rack and service of marmalade and preserves nearer the customer
- ask if more toast, coffee or a fresh pot of tea is required

Breakfast waiting procedures

Follow all general service rules especially in regard to:

- removing unwanted cover silver after orders have been taken
- accompaniments, for example caster sugar sifter with grapefruit, compotes, etc., mustard with fried and grilled items
- replenishing beverages, toast, and butter as required
- tea and toast being freshly made, coffee and hot milk really hot (customers rightly blame the waiter if they are not; for he is responsible for checking that items are freshly made and hot)

Re-laying at breakfast

Re-laying tables in a busy breakfast room may be eased by a system of prepared trays containing all the mise en place for this purpose. Stack sideboards with cutlery, plates, cups, saucers, napkins, condiments, sauces, sugars, large and small tablecloths, as may be required during service. The breakfast buffet laid at one point in the room with cereals, iced water, chilled fruit juices in glass jugs with glasses available, fruit, etc. also relieves the problem.

Delay and complaining

Never keep the customer unnecessarily waiting between courses. Refer any delay in food service to the head waiter. He should investigate and seek to remedy any delay, apologize to the guest, and explain that he is seeking to overcome it.

Breakfast billing

Pass checks and bills promptly to the cashier as guests may leave immediately after breakfast and items will not be paid for unless added to the bill.

Floor service breakfast

Because of high cost, floor service is more rarely offered than formerly and is largely confined to luxurious, high-priced hotels. Floor breakfasts are usually ordered:

- the previous night on cards completed by the guest and then affixed to the door handle outside the room
- through the night porter
- by standing order
- by phoning through to room service

Floor waiters use trays and trolleys in serving breakfasts in rooms. Usually trays are used for single orders and trolleys for an order for two persons.

- Lay these with china and cutlery the previous night in the floor pantry
- At the last minute place any hot food and beverage on the tray or trolley and take it to the customer at the requested time
- Knock at the guest's door and wait to be admitted
- On entry, place the tray on a special side-table (only on the bed if the guest so asks)
- If a trolley is used, wheel it into the room and place either in the centre, by the window, or by the bed as requested by the guest
- Show the dishes brought to the guest in case the order is incorrect or not to his liking. (It can then be changed without the guest having to ring for the waiter again)
- When about to leave, ask if anything else is required, otherwise do not enter the room again unless called for

Laying a tray

Trays in hotels are generally used only for serving meals in bedrooms and private suites or for afternoon teas (see Figure 40).

For the service of a meal in bed, lay-up is the same as for laying a table; in most cases the tray will be placed on the bed, or a trestle, as a table.

For service in sitting rooms, lay a table in the same style as in a restaurant.

Carrying a tray

- Balance a tray on your outspread palm level with your shoulder (see Figure 41) so that your right hand is free to knock on the door and then to open it on obtaining permission to enter
- When it is to be carried, lay in such a way that the heaviest dishes are in the centre, with glasses and lighter articles towards the edges of the tray. Place the glasses upside down for stability
- In a restaurant, do not carry bottles of wine or mineral waters on trays,

Figure 40   A tray layed for breakfast.

except wine bottles in cradles or wine coolers. However, lounge waiters often carry split-size minerals on their trays

- Do not take two hot courses on the same tray at the same time to the same room; the second course is likely to get cold while the first is being eaten

Trays are used in all branches of catering. Some cafeterias, cafés and canteens bring food courses to customers on trays and place the tray on the table in front of the guest. In such cases, arrange and carry trays in accordance with the general instructions above.

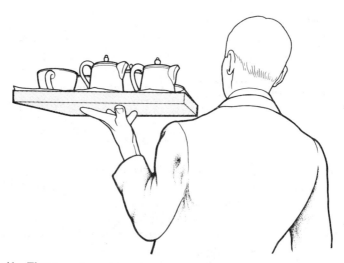

Figure 41   The correct way to carry a tray.

Floor breakfast clearance

Often the tray or trolley is left for the chamber maid to clear when she is cleaning the room. She places it either in the passage or in the floor pantry for the waiter to clear later. Ordinarily he sends dirty plates down the lift but retains cutlery, pots and cups to wash himself. These latter are usually his stock, kept in the pantry.

Floor pantry or service room

Main meals for floor service may be sent from the main kitchens. Breakfast and subsidiary services, however, may be finally prepared and cooked in a floor pantry or service room. Procedures and scope of preparation vary, for instance whether or not a pantry maid or floor attendant assists or chambermaids are involved. Often the floor-service room is run by floor waiting staff.

Used items, for example plates, are ordinarily returned to the wash-up by lift, but cutlery, pots and cups from floor stock may be retained for washing by waiting staff in this pantry. Thus, the floor pantry is provided with a sink, a lift to stillroom and kitchen, and simple heating or cooking apparatus to boil water and keep beverages hot. Tea and other hot beverages may come from the stillroom, but more commonly dry tea and a supply of hot coffee and milk are sent up to the floor pantry.

A communication system (telephone or intercom) will link the floor service room with stillroom or kitchen.

Floor service of afternoon tea

Serving afternoon tea on the floors is similar to the room service of breakfast described previously. A stock of afternoon crockery and cutlery is kept in the floor pantry, where the tea is usually made. Food items are sent from the stillroom by service lift. Tea service is described in Chapter 17.

Floor checking

Checking for floor service is usually effected through 'floor' pads of different colour from the dining room. Carefully and clearly mark the room numbers as floor service usually involves an additional charge to the guest. Pass duplicate checks down to the cashier as soon as possible for many guests leave immediately after receiving service.

17
Coffee, Tea and Lounge Service

Guests may order coffee with every meal: breakfast, luncheon and dinner. Tea is also important because it is often demanded at breakfast and in the afternoon with afternoon tea or high tea or as a beverage. Both coffee and tea are, additionally, often ordered mid-morning or indeed at any time of the day or evening when refreshment is required.

The stillroom (cafeterie)

In many establishments tea is made by a stillroom maid or service counterhand. The waiter is concerned only with serving it. The stillroom, where tea, coffee and similar beverages are prepared, is traditionally supervised by the restaurant manager or maître d'hôtel rather than the chef de cuisine. In this department are similarly prepared toasts (plain and Melba), butter pats and, often, sandwiches at time of larder closure.

Coffee

Coffee-making

Because of stillroom links with waiting staff, the fundamentals of coffee should be understood. Moreover, coffee is often infused in the restaurant by filters, percolators and other devices. Coffee should be strong without being bitter, dark but bright in colour and full flavoured with a pleasant aroma. For a balanced coffee, observe the following.

- Make freshly, never more than half an hour or so before serving. Coffee kept too long or re-heated loses its brightness and flavour.
- Keep appliances clean. Coffee takes other flavours easily and good maintenance of apparatus is essential.
- Use the same blend of coffee at the correct grind.
- Weigh or measure ground coffee for the liquid required (guesswork

can cause flavour to fluctuate from meal to meal). A guide is 225 g (8 oz) to 4½ litres (one gallon) of water.

- When making coffee, or keeping coffee hot, never boil or simmer. (Boiling extracts harsh qualities and causes bitterness.)
- Although boiling water is used in making coffee, the apparatus is so designed that the temperature drops to just below boiling, 98°C (208°F) before infusion with the grind.
- Made coffee is usually kept at about 82°C (180°F).
- Heat pots and cups before serving to guard against tepid coffee.
- If fresh cream is preferred to milk, pour it gently onto the coffee so that it floats.

Vacuum infusion method (heat-resisting glass)

- Place the correct measure of medium-grind coffee (one heaped teaspoon to each small coffee cup to full capacity of bowl) in the funnel with the glass stopper already in position.
- Fill the bowl to 2.5 cm (1 inch) from the top with boiling water.
- Fix the funnel firmly into the bowl with a slight twist to ensure that the join is air-tight and the lighted methylated lamp placed underneath.
- The boiling water is forced up the funnel tube and infuses with the grounds.
- Leave it for 1 minute. If some of the grind does not mix, stir lightly but take care not to touch the stopper.
- Remove the lamp and the coffee will descend into the bowl. If the descent is retarded, it will be due to an airlock. Clear it by placing the lamp under again and sending the coffee back up, giving a slight extra twist to the cork and allowing the coffee to descend again.
- When all the coffee has dropped into the bowl, remove the funnel (with a reverse twist) and serve coffee from the bowl.
- For efficiency, always use the machines to capacity (they are made in various sizes, select the appropriate one).

Electric simmerstats

Larger machines in batteries in strategic positions in the room for regular coffee supply work on the same principle as table models, but can be ready slightly in advance and kept at correct temperatures by controlled heat.

Café filtre

Among many devices for coffee-making, the traditional filter consists of a French, brown pot, topped by an infusion pot filled with filter ground coffee. Add boiling water and leave to percolate through to the pot beneath. Remove the infuser pot, replace with a lid and serve the coffee.

There are many adaptations for individual service using the filter or drip method, all basically the same. Coffee in a filter funnel fits on top of the pot, glass, or cup, through which the brew slowly percolates.

Breakfast coffee

There are two main alternative forms of breakfast coffee service.

Traditional Place coffee, milk and sugar on the table in a coffee pot, milk jug and sugar bowl. Customers help themselves as they do in their own homes. When several people in one party occupy a table, place the coffee service on the right of the senior or eldest lady present.

Pour 'n' serve Coffee is brewed on a sideboard or table in a simmerstat (Cona or similar) machine. With an accompanying jug of hot milk, this is carried from table to table by the waiter.

Main meal coffee

After luncheon or dinner, coffee should be served by the waiter. Prior to coffee service, when all guests have finished eating:

- once again clear and crumb the table
- remove dirty and empty glasses (but do not remove glasses not emptied without guest's consent)
- a napperon (small, clean white cloth), in some cases, is laid on the table to cover any stains made during the meal
- place a clean ashtray on the table
- place a small coffee cup and saucer on a china plate with the coffee spoon at an angle so that the handle points to the customer's right hand
- set this service from the left in front of each guest

Traditional service (Figure 42)

- On the palm of your left hand carry a doyley-covered plate (or tray with doyley or cloth), set with coffee pot, milk jug and sugar bowl
- Make sure that the coffee and milk are really hot
- Go to the right of the guest and enquire ('will you have black coffee, sir, or with milk?' (Avoid the slang expression 'white' when you mean coffee with milk. It is not always understood by overseas visitors)
- Then enquire 'do you take sugar, please sir?' and if so 'how many lumps?' (or spoonfuls if brown, for example, is the guest's choice)
- Serve the coffee by tilting the pot, filling the cup with coffee to a third of a centimetre from the brim. (In the best service, incline the coffee pot in a downwards position making a pivot of the part of the pot exactly under the spout, but so that this pivotal point does not leave the tray or plate; this requires practice)
- If milk is required, similarly serve from the milk jug
- Having served sugar separately first, you may leave the bowl on the table
- When service is completed, place coffee pot and milk jug on the table at the host's right

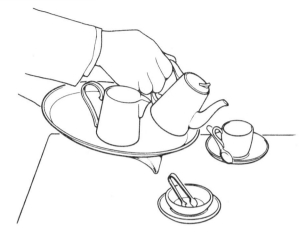

Figure 42 Traditional service of coffee. The waiter/waitress inclines the pot downwards, making a pivot of the part of the base exactly under the spout. The pivot point remains on the tray.

Modern coffee service

Since traditional practice can be difficult (even dangerous, especially for inexperienced waiters), a modern alternative is to lift the pots or jugs one at a time, holding each firmly. In any case, service style will be decided upon by management as appropriate to customer requirements, staff capabilities and economics.

'Pour 'n serve' from electric simmerstat machines (Figure 43), referred to earlier, is also used in some operations at main meal times as well as breakfast.

Turkish coffee

Turkish coffee is a special service with tiny cups, half the size of a demi-tasse and brewed in a metal, long-handled coffee pot.

- Take a teaspoon of very finely ground coffee for each Turkish coffee cup
- Three-quarters fill the special Turkish, long-handled coffee pot with water
- Bring to the boil over a spirit lamp
- Withdraw from the heat
- Add the coffee (very finely ground for Turkish coffee)
- Return to the flame, but again withdraw as soon as the coffee starts to rise, and allow to settle
- Repeat this process twice more

Figure 43   A Cona coffee machine.

- Finally, sprinkle in a few drops of cold water (a drop or two of rose water may also be added) but gently so as not to disperse the froth (this cold sprinkle ensures that the grounds subside)

At one time this service was effected by costumed attendants.

Other speciality coffees

Speciality coffees served after main meals consist of hot black coffee, spirit (or liqueur) with cream floated on the surface (Table 11). Presentation is in a glass. If not heat-proof, place a coffee spoon in the glass when pouring in the hot coffee to guard against cracking or breaking the glass.

Unless unsweetened coffee is required, first place Demerara sugar into the glass, then a measure of the required spirit or liqueur. Pour in hot black coffee to within 2 cm ($\frac{3}{4}$ inch) of the rim. Stir and then float on cold double cream by pouring gently over a teaspoon, held bowl uppermost, just above the surface of the coffee.

Table 11   Examples of speciality coffees.

Name	Added spirit/liqueur
Calypso	Tia Maria
French	Brandy
Gaelic	Scotch whisky
Irish	Irish whiskey

Monks	Benedictine
Prince Charles	Drambuie
Russian	Vodka

Liqueurs

Liqueurs are usually served into the glass and carried on a silver salver to the table.

- Place at the right of the coffee cup, but not near the edge of the table
- Appropriately vary this procedure if there is a liqueur trolley service

(See Chapter 18 for further information about liqueurs and drinks.)

Tea

Tea is demanded less frequently than coffee at luncheon or dinner in high-class restaurants; however, tea may sometimes be asked for in place of coffee at a meal's conclusion.

Tea in place of coffee

If, after a main meal, a guest requires a pot of tea:

- place a small tea cup, teaspoon and saucer on a side plate in front of him
- place a small tray with a teapot, hot water jug, and milk jug at his right hand side for him to help himself whenever he judges the tea to be sufficiently infused
- never, as waiter, pour tea into the cup (except at buffet teas; pp. 178–9)

Teapots

Tea is best made and served in teapots, preferably earthenware with non-drip spouts. Silver or plated pots are also suitable, but clean and dry them after use, otherwise they stain and become musty. Store teapots with separate lids upside down with the lid off to drain away moisture and keep the teapot 'sweet'. Store those with hinged lids, such as silver teapots, with the lid closed.

Tea brewing

- Use good tea. High-quality blends produce better tea.
- Use freshly-drawn, freshly boiled water. Water 'stales' if allowed to stand. Never re-use water that has been boiled for tea-making. Water which has not come to the boil causes tea to be flat.

- Warm the pot. Water poured into a cold pot goes off the boil and the tea will not be so good.
- 'Short pour'. For full benefit, water should reach the tea leaves as near boiling point as possible. Take the teapot to the kettle and not the kettle to the teapot. If, as is more likely, a boiler is being used, make sure the teapots are brought right up to the boiling water outlet.
- Brew, but do not stew. Allow 4–6 minutes for infusion, depending upon the size of the pot and the nature of the water. The larger the pot, the longer the time for infusion; soft water infuses tea more readily than hard water.

If tea is being served in cups, put the tea in the cup before the milk is added. However hurried the service, never put milk in the teapot or urn.

Lounge waiting

Lounge waiting duties vary according to house custom. In addition to serving refreshments, a lounge waiter ensures that lounge tables and other appointments are clean and tidy throughout his spell of duty, and magazines (if provided), cushions, etc. are neatly arranged.

Ashtrays

Keep an eye on ashtrays, replacing used ones with clean ones. To do this:

- invert the clean ashtray over the used one on the table
- remove both together, the clean one concealing the soiled one
- when both are well clear of the table, place the clean ashtray on the table

Always be aware of guests' needs, but though your duty is to sell, avoid over-attentiveness, that is, do not give residents who may wish to sit quietly any feeling of obligation to order.

Tea meals

Teas include:

> *set teas*: afternoon teas and high teas
> *à la carte*: afternoon teas and high teas
> *tea receptions*

In hotels, afternoon teas are served from about 3.45 – 5 pm in the lounge.

Lounge preparation for tea

About 1 hour before service, cover the lounge tables with tablecloths. Lay on each: a flower vase, ashtray, two, three or four teacups and saucers with teaspoons, lump sugar basin and tongs, slop basin with tea strainer, small tea plates. Place a small knife to the right and a pastry fork to the left of each plate and a small folded tea napkin on each plate. A lighter type of china, often with a floral pattern, may be used for afternoon tea.

Afternoon tea items

Menus are not usually provided for a set afternoon tea; however one example of such a menu is given in Figure 44.

Figure 44 An afternoon tea menu, The Savoy.

Afternoon teas may include a selection from the following.

Sandwiches: Small and dainty of brown and white bread and butter; light fillings such as fish and meat spreads or pastes, cucumber, egg and cress, lettuce, tomato and, less commonly, meat, chicken, smoked salmon.
Bread and butter: White, wholemeal, currant, malt and proprietory.
Scones and buns: Tea cakes, scones, buns (Chelsea, Bath, etc.); Scotch pancakes, Sally Lunns, etc. for service with butter.

Toasted items: Plain buttered toast and/or crumpets, muffins, teacakes, buns, etc.

Preserves: Honey, jam, lemon curd (but not usually marmalade).

Beverages: Indian, China, Ceylon teas – with milk or lemon, or Russian style. Overseas guests may select chocolate, coffee or other milk and non-alcoholic beverages.

Cakes and pastries: Apart from traditional items such as fruit cake, Madeira, sponges and other plainer cakes, further items are indicated in the examples which follow.

French pastries: Some gâteaux, desserts and biscuits for sweet courses may be used, e.g. savarins, flans, bandes de fruit, small babas, meringue, etc.

French pastries

The following short list provides a few examples of French pastries.

Gâteaux (Genoise based) for cutting

Champignons: Genoise sandwiches with vanilla butter cream, almond nibs on side, topped with chocolate powder-dusted meringues in mushroom shapes.

Daumier: Two pink and two plain genoise strips joined in contrasting colour by apricot jam to form a rectangular gâteau, marzipan covered; slices have checkered effect.

Moka: Genoise sandwiches coated with coffee cream, with toasted almond nibs on side, and a piped top.

Nelusko: Genoise sandwiched with praliné butter cream, glazed with chocolate fondant icing. Word 'Nelusko' piped on in white icing or butter cream.

Pâtisseries (small pastries)

Some small pastries are cut from gâteaux, for example daumiers, mille feuilles; or some are miniature versions of gâteaux, for example conversations, chocolatines. From the many possibilities, the following are a few examples.

Barquettes grillées: Boat-shaped tartlettes, filled with almond cream, two puff paste strips criss-crossed on top; iced with plain icing. (Other barquettes may be provided with flan-type fillings.)

Boules de Berlin (Berlin balls):   (Doughnuts.) Savarin-type mix, moulded with jam centre, deep fried, rolled in cinnamon sugar.

Chaussons: Puff paste turnovers (e.g. chaussons de pommes, apple turnovers; chaussons de confiture, jam turnovers).

Conversations: Puff paste tartlets, almond cream filling, two puff paste strips criss-crossed on top.

Cornets à la crème: Puff paste cornets filled with chantilly cream (sometimes also a little raspberry jam).

Éclairs: Choux paste fingers filled with crème pâtissière and iced with coffee fondant (éclairs café) or chocolate fondant (éclairs chocolat). In Britain crème chantilly is often used in lieu of pastry cream.

Gaufrettes viennoises: Vienna wafers. Squares of short paste incorporating ground almonds, sandwiched with raspberry jam. (Top, knife-patterned in diamonds and piped with icing before baking.)

Linzer: Short paste with ground almonds, spread raspberry jam, covered with lattice strips of paste before baking. Cut in shape as desired.

Madeleines: Small, plain, vanilla, egg sponges.

Meringues chantilly: Meringue sandwiched with chantilly cream.

Nougatines: Meringue-type mix with ground almonds, baked in variety of piped shapes.

Pains de Gênes: Shortbread-type mix incorporating ground almonds, egg, rum (or liqueur), baked in small plain or fancy moulds. Icing sugar sprinkled.

Sables: Shortcakes or shortbread, any shape.

Serving afternoon tea

When taking the order, inquire whether Indian, China or Russian tea is required and whether with milk or lemon. Bring from the stillroom the pot of tea, hot water, milk, cream or lemon on a silver tray. Place the pot of tea and hot water on the table on small plates or stands (with the milk conveniently close) in front of the senior lady to allow her to pour out the tea. If coffee and milk is ordered, similarly place the pots on the table. If only gentlemen are present, find out tactfully who wishes to pour.

For a set tea (or as may be ordered à la carte), bring buttered scones, tea cakes or toast, and a variety of small sandwiches.

After these have been consumed, change the plates and pass pastries (either on a trolley or a large silver tray). Offer also cut cakes such as Dundee and Madeira. Gâteaux and pastries are usually served with a flat gâteau slice.

Other orders

During the summer, some customers may order iced coffee or tea. Serve in large glasses, full of crushed ice, with lemon for tea and cream for coffee.

Ices, ice-cream or strawberries may also be ordered as extras instead of a tea.

High tea or à la carte tea

High tea, a more substantial afternoon meal, is served in popular restaurants and cafés rather than in hotels. Items such as a pot or cup of tea, bread, butter, jam, cakes, fish and chips, etc. may be charged separately or a set tea offered at a fixed price, any extra being charged.

Superior establishments may affect to despise high tea. Indeed, as a blend of food and beverage it can hardly be defended on gastronomic grounds. Nevertheless, in Britain 'tea' often means a meal. There remains substantial demand for this late afternoon meal with tea and cooked (hot or cold) meat, fish, poultry, etc. items.

Lay-up is normally as for breakfast. Service procedure is as for afternoon tea except that the service of sweet items may be deferred until the 'main' course has been completed.

High tea dishes

Typical items served at high tea are:

Eggs: Boiled, poached or scrambled on toast, fried with French fried potatoes, omelets.

Savouries: Substantial size portion of Welsh Rarebit, Buck Rarebit, baked beans on toast, spaghetti, mushrooms on toast.

Fish: Cold lobster, salmon salads, dressed crab, or a wide range of fried, grilled, baked fish usually with chipped potatoes.

Meats: Cold buffet items, grilled steaks, chops, mixed grills, brunch, sausages, grilled or even roast chicken usually with French fries and/or grilled tomatoes, mushrooms, etc.

Sweets: In addition to gâteaux and pastries, a sweet course may also be served. Items could include ices, coupes, sundaes, splits, fruit salad, compotes, cold fruit tarts and pies, mousses, bavarois, jellies and other cold (seldom hot) desserts.

Tea receptions

For reception teas served from a buffet, put tables together to form a raised buffet by supporting the legs on boxes. Lay buffet cloths so as just to touch the floor all round. Pin the cloths with straight creases for neat corners.

Arrange small, teacloth-covered lounge tables laid with ashtrays and vases of flowers about the room and chairs around the walls. Just before guests arrive, lay the buffet. Typical selections include finger sandwiches (such as sardine, chicken, ham, tomato, cucumber, mustard and cress, egg, anchovy paste); and if of higher cost caviar, foie gras, smoked salmon sandwiches, also bouchées and canapés; pastries, sponges, gâteaux, jellies, blancmange and other sweet items.

Add sufficient plates, forks and dessert silver for both savoury and sweet items. Set cups, saucers, teaspoons and sugar ready for service near the urns of freshly brewed tea. (Coffee and milk may also be available.) Hot beverages may stand on a hotplate; alternatively insulated pots may be used.

Staff service

With enough crockery and cutlery for speedy service and with everything en place beforehand, as above, half a dozen staff can service a reception of several hundred.

Guests help themselves but waiters:

- pour tea (or coffee) and milk
- stand by to clear and assist
- replenish the buffet (ladies or the elderly who may prefer to sit at the table are waited on by their escorts)

Pouring tea

At buffet teas and similar occasions, waiting staff may pour tea. Whilst recognizing that many people may first pour milk into the cup, the rule (unless otherwise requested by a guest) is to pour tea first, then add milk and leave guests to add their own sugar.

18
Wine, Drinks and Tobacco

Fine wine needs care in storage and service; thus a wine waiter must know about cellar conditions and how to serve the various wines.

Storages

- Cellars should be away from the main thoroughfare to minimize the risk of vibration, if possible underground
- Average cellar temperature should be 13°C (55°F)
- Avoid continual changes of temperature, which affects wine
- Bottled wine, once binned, should not be disturbed until required for service, therefore:
    store each type and vintage separately
    correctly number each section of the binning space for
    easy location of the wine
    ensure that these numbers correspond with those on the wine list
- Where red and white wines have to be stored in the same room, keep red wines in the upper bins (warmer temperature) and white wines in the lower bins (cooler temperature)

Glasses

The shape and type of glass helps to bring out the colour, aroma and taste of wine. A wine glass should be of good clear glass, slightly curved at the top to form a tulip shape so that the aroma is trapped for the nose to appreciate. The glass should be thin; for thick glassware spoils the pleasure in wine drinking.

Many operations adopt a standard size of glass 1.5 – 2.25 dl (6 – 8 oz) for all table wines. The tulip shape, or alternatively the Paris goblet, is most favoured, yielding approximately six glasses per bottle of wine.

Champagne flutes are widely used as also are champagne coupes or saucers, though these latter are not approved by connoisseurs.

Good brandy is served in balloon glasses in many establishments, but again connoisseurs deplore their being excessively large.

Setting glasses on the table

During the general setting of the room, the wine waiter places an all-purpose goblet at each cover. These goblets are carried upside down between the fingers of the left hand. The method of loading and unloading glasses carried in this way is important as breakages occur if not properly carried out.

Train yourself to carry glasses in this way as it is a quicker and safer way of transferring them from the pantry shelf to the tables.

Always carry tumblers on salvers.

During service and clearance

During meal service, however, always carry glasses the right way up on salvers (round trays 30 cm (12 inches) in diameter, having a concave edge) whether they are being set on a table or cleared.

Place the glass on the table at the right side of the cover at the outside tip of the large knife; or if there is not a large knife, then just where it would normally be placed.

If it is necessary to change a glass, bring the fresh glass on a salver to the table and exchange the glasses by picking up the table glass and putting on the tray and placing the fresh glass in its place.

Remember the following points.

- Remove glasses from the table when empty
- Serve fresh wines (even if a second bottle of the same wine is ordered) and other drinks in fresh glasses
- Handle glasses by the stem (between thumb and fingers), or for the tumbler type, low down near the base
- Never pick up or clear glasses by putting the fingers inside
- Bring clean glasses into the room during service only when required so that they can go straight onto the table
- Remove dirty glasses on a salver or tray, straightaway take them to the glass pantry
- Carry glasses on their own, never place them out of sight under a sideboard.
- Broken glass in a room can be dangerous; be cautious therefore in handling glassware

Function glasses

When laying banquet covers, place three or more glasses, for example sherry, claret and/or hock and champagne, in order of use, the smallest glass to the right. Above them on the table, place a port glass and a liqueur glass.

Glassware

Glass commonly used for wine and drink service includes:

Water or wine goblet	Capacity 2.25 dl (8 oz)
Claret glass	Capacity 1.5 dl (6 oz)
Sherry glass	Capacity 0.75 – 1.0 dl (3 – 4 oz)
Port glass	Capacity 1 dl (4 oz)
Liqueur glass	Capacity usually very small
Hock glass	Tulip shape, amber coloured, long stem
Moselle glass	Tulip shape, green coloured, long stem
Burgundy balloon	Large glass for fine burgundy wines
Champagne tulip	Tall, slender glass
Champagne coupe or saucer	Straight side, wide at top (traditional but not now fashionable)
Cocktail glass	Varies in shape
Lager glass	May be tall, flute type or stemmed 'hock' type
Brandy balloon	Large glass with narrow opening and short stem

Other containers include:

Jugs for water and beer
Silver or pewter tankards in 3 dl (½ pint) (and possibly 6 dl (1 pint)) measure for draught beer and bottled beer other than lager

Ordering wine

Wine sales in licensed restaurants yield profit. For the high-class restaurant it is a 'must', since a meal is not complete without wine. Therefore, present the wine list (Figure 45) at each table (from the left hand side of the customer) at the proper time; that is, when food has been ordered. Thereafter, ensure that the wine is served correctly.

Writing a wine check

When the order has been given write out a cellar check. This is usually with two carbon copies: the original sent to the cellar or dispense to obtain the bottle; the duplicate to the cashier; and the third copy to the station waiter for reference and comparison with the bill when it is presented.

Wines are ordered by numbers in most establishments. In the wine list, to the right of the description of the wine, are two columns showing the price of whole and half bottles. Thus, the check, illustrated in Figure 46, for an order taken by waiter W.O., would read 1 × 57 or ½ × 57 according to the customer's requirements, the price being altered accordingly.

WINE AND BEVERAGE PRICE LIST

DRINKS TARIFF

Gin, rum, vodka and whisky are offered for sale on these premises in quantities of one-sixth of a gill or in multiples thereof.

SPIRITS

Gin, Whisky, Rum, Vodka	£0.95
Whisky, Malt or Deluxe	£1.00
Barcadi	£0.95
Brandy xxx	£1.10
Brandy VSOP	£1.35
Advocaat	£0.95
Liqueurs	£1.00

VERMOUTH, PORTS, SHERRIES

Vermouth, Dubonnet	£0.95
Pernod	£1.05
Campari	£1.25
Port, Calem Vintage Character (Glass)	£1.05
Fonseca Vintage Port '70 (Glass)	£1.40
Fiesta Sherry, dry, medium or sweet	£0.90
Tio Pepe	£0.95

MINERALS

Baby (when served with spirits)	£0.35
Mineral Water	£0.65
Pepsi Cola	£0.50
Fruit Cup (non-alcoholic) jug for four	£2.95
Cider	£0.65
Fruit Juice and other soft drinks	£0.70

WINE

Arc de Triomphe red or white (glass) 125 ml	£1.15

BOTTLED BEER

Double Diamond	£0.65
Guiness Stout	£0.75
Carlsberg	£0.90

DRAUGHT BEER

	Per Pint	Per ½ pint
Bitter	£1.00	£0.50
Lager	£1.10	£0.55

A selection of spirits is available by the bottle with mixers, served to your table – Prices on application

WINE LIST

		Bottle	½ Bottle
HOUSE WINES (Produce of France)			
Cuvee De Patron			
Medium dry white or full and mellow red (LB)		£6.25	£3.30

Bin No.		Bottle	½ Bottle
WHITE			
20.	Frascati Superiore D.O.C. 1983/4 (IB)	£7.15	—
21.	Liebfraumilch Wedding Veil Qualitatswein (GB)	£7.25	£3.85
22.	Muscadet Cuvee Madeleine Sevre et Maine 1983/4 (FB)	£7.40	—
23.	Niersteiner Gutes Domthal Spatlese Qualitatswein 1983 (GB)	£8.95	—
24.	Macon Blanc Villages Jaboulet-Vercherre 1982/3 (FB)	£9.95	—
RED			
30.	Valpolicella D.O.C. Paolo Boscaini (IB)	£6.50	—
31.	Cotes du Rhone Paul Deloux 1984 (LB)	£7.10	£3.75
32.	Claret Bordeaux (LB)	£7.20	—
33.	Mouton Cadet Selection Rothschild (FB)	£8.95	—
34.	Beaujolais Villages 1983/4 Louis Latour (FB)	£9.75	—
ROSE			
40.	Mateus Rose (PB)	£7.35	£3.85
SPARKLING WINES AND CHAMPAGNE			
50.	Asti Spumante D.O.C. Calamandrana (IB)	£8.20	—
51.	Ayala Chateau d'Ay Extra Dry N.V. (FB)	£14.25	—

When stocks of any particular vintage become exhausted the best succeeding one is offered with every confidence.

Bottled in: France (FB), Germany (GB), London (LB), Italy (IB), Portugal (PB)

All prices are inclusive of service and Value Added Tax

STRAND PALACE HOTEL
Strand
London WC2R 0JJ
Telephone: 01-836 8080
Telex: 24208

STRAND PALACE HOTEL

Figure 45 An example of a wine list, The Strand Palace Hotel.

Presentation procedure

When the bottle has been obtained, present it to the customer, from the latter's right hand side, at a suitable angle so that he can easily read the label. Mention the name of the wine and vintage, if any, for example 'Your Chateau Latour 1978, sir'.

Take care not to shake the wine (for this may disturb any sediment) nor to shake any dust from the bottle on the table.

	Table No.
	15
1 x 57	740p
Date 9/3/86	Sig. W.O.

Figure 46   An example of a check taken for a wine order.

Cork removal (Figure 47)

When the customer has approved the wine, leave the table, remove any wax, or cut the tinfoil round the bottle's lip, carefully wipe the lip of the bottle (or some sediment may drop in the glass later), and draw the cork.

The best corkscrew for the wine waiter is the lever ('the waiter's friend') or the French boxwood corkscrew. Correct use allows the cork to be drawn quietly and smoothly without breaking the neck of the bottle.

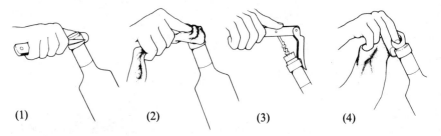

(1)   (2)   (3)   (4)

Figure 47   Uncorking a wine bottle. (1) Cut through the foil around the top of the bottle's neck and remove. This ensures that when the wine is poured it does not come into contact with the foil. (2) Wipe the top of the neck and mouth with a clean dry cloth. (3) Insert the corkscrew and use leverage on the bottle-neck's rim to draw. (4) Carefully wipe the mouth.

- Do not drive the screw right through the cork or pieces may fall into the wine
- Pull the cork to within 0.35 cm to 1.25 cm of the end and then withdraw with a slight twist, by the thumb and fingers. This allays any last minute jerk and allows air to take the place of the cork more steadily
- Never hold a bottle between your legs when drawing a cork
- Cover the forefinger of your right hand with the corner of a waiter's (clean) cloth, insert it in the opening of the neck of the bottle (meanwhile holding the bottle steady in the left hand) and gently wipe inside, in case there is any vestige of cork there
- The wine is ready to be served

Serving the wine

- First pour a little wine into the host's glass for him to sample the wine (Figure 48).
- When approved, continue serving the wine beginning at the right of the host with the ladies, then from the right again with the gentlemen until the host is again reached and the service completed.
- Pour wine carefully and steadily.
- Hold the bottle (label uppermost so that it can be read) with the hand over the bottle, the thumb round one side, the fingers round the other, and the index finger lying up the shoulder (not on the neck).
- Place the lip of the bottle just over the edge of the glass and then tip downwards with a movement of the wrist until the wine begins to flow. In this way pouring is under control and can be stopped by just moving the hand upwards, again by pivoting from the wrist.
- At the end of each pouring, remove possible drips by touching the lip of the bottle with a waiter's cloth folded into a pad.

Figure 48   Serving wine. When held in this position, the bottle is properly balanced. Note the position of the first finger, well back from the neck of the bottle.

Corky wine

Before serving a wine smell the cork carefully. If you detect any unpleasant odour, indicating that the cork has gone musty and the mustiness has been absorbed by the wine, at once either replace the bottle by another or report the fact to the head waiter or manager. (Most good wine merchants replace corky bottles.)

Service of white wines

- Serve white wines slightly chilled at about 10°C (50°F). Modern equipment allows wines to be at correct temperatures for service, but in some cases this is not so, or a customer may like his wine colder.
- Place the wine in a wine cooler, with water and ice just to the shoulder of the bottle.
- Place the wine cooler in a stand at the side of the table, or on a large plate (on which has been placed a napkin) which can be put on the table. Wine coolers are, however, intended for keeping the remainder of the wine cool after first service. A deeper receptacle is essential for the proper cooling of a bottle of white or sparkling wine.
- After presentation, remove the cork with a lever screw without taking the wine from the cooler.
- When offering the host the sample to taste, ask if the temperature of the wine is satisfactory.
- If it is not cool enough, ask the host if he would like a little poured out or if he would prefer all the wine to be returned to the cooler for another few minutes.
- When the wine has been served, ask the host if he would like the wine left in the bottle replaced in the cooler or left out, as it may now be chilled sufficiently.
- Take care that wine is not over-iced for the aroma can then be masked.
- With white wines, pour no more than two-thirds of a glass.
- When placing a bottle on the table, put it just above and to the left of the host's wine glass with the label facing him.
- Keep constant contact; re-fill the glasses when necessary.
- When the bottle is empty, politely inform the host that the wine is finished. The host can then order more wine if he thinks fit.
- Place a napkin at the wine cooler for the purpose of wiping the bottle each time it is taken out. Do not use this napking for wiping the neck of the bottle when serving the wine.

Service of red wines

Serve red wines at room temperature, about 18°C (65°F). Most establishments have sufficient red wine stored near the room for this purpose.

Decanting

Old red wines have a sediment and must be handled carefully or this will be disturbed. For these old reds, a wine waiter, on receiving the order, may recommend decanting. On some wine lists, it is stated that all red wines over a certain age will be decanted unless the customer wishes otherwise. Politely point this out to save repercussions if the customer is offended through having his wine opened before presentation. For least disturbance, it is better to decant in the cellar. Heavy decanters are generally used for old port; other wines are decanted into more delicate carafes. Before serving, present the original bottle and cork to the customer to assure him that the wine he has chosen is, in fact, being served.

Wine cradles

Should a customer insist on the wine being served from the bottle, the cellarman will place the bottle in a wine cradle. Draw the cork with care and only after the bottle has been presented at the table. A lever corkscrew is of value in removing corks from bottles in cradles for corks can be crumbly after so many years.

Younger red wines which have not had time to gain a sediment do not need decanting; however handle them with grace as you should with all wines.

Temperature and breathing

Should a customer complain that a red wine is not 'roomed' and he requires it 'chambré' (French for roomed), never immerse the bottle in hot water, nor stand it in front of a fire, nor place it on a hot-plate. Such action kills the fine quality and bouquet of the wine and sends it cloudy. As the only safe method is to raise the temperature gradually, the head waiter should be informed.

The least drastic method is to warm a decanter and carefully pour in the wine so that it gathers the warmth as it fills.

In residential hotels, get to know your guests and take wine orders during the previous meal, so that red wines can be placed in the room well in advance. Another point in favour of this is that the cork can be drawn to allow the wine to breathe. This assists an old red wine, for it has been imprisoned for a long time.

Do not pour more than half a glass of any red wine, so that the aromas can expand and be enjoyed.

Champagne and other sparkling wines

Serve sparkling wines chilled. They are often appreciated more chilled than still white wines.

Handle champagne bottles gently. Agitation of the bottle before opening causes increased effervescence, that is, 'fizz', which impedes good service.

After presentation, not forgetting to mention vintage (if any), draw the cork.

- Do not allow the bottle to point in the guests' direction when drawing the cork.
- Hold the bottle in the left hand.
- Remove the wire at the point indicated on the gold foil (generally a piece of twisted wire), with the right hand, by a slight twisting movement.
- Place a cloth over the hand gripping the bottle while the cork is extracted.

- Have quick access to the host's glass, for the wine may surge out of the bottle. With near access to the glass, you can quickly incline the bottle over the glass, preventing any spillage.
- Smell the cork before other guests are served. If the bottle is 'corky' remove the host's glass with the bottle and substitute another.

Service sequence (see Table 12)

Table 12   Wines with courses.

Wine	Course
Graves or Chablis	Oysters
Sherry, Marsala, Madeira	Soup
Hock, Moselle, Sauterne or Chablis	Fish
Claret, Burgundy, Chianti or Champagne	Relevé, entrée roasts and entremets
Port	Cheese
Port, Madeira, Marsala or Malaga	Fruit
Brandy and liqueurs	Coffee or later

Serving a different wine with each course tends to be confined nowadays to formal occasions. A sherry might be served with the soup course, after which any one of the table wines mentioned in Table 12 may be served with the remainder of the meal.

Generally, dry wines come first and sweet wines last; if a dry wine is served after a sweet wine it will taste too dry (i.e. sour), whereas a sweet wine, coming after dry wine, tastes sweeter.

Sequence summarized

When in doubt serve:

- dry wines before sweet wines
- young wines before old wines
- white wines before red wines

Hints to wine waiters

- Never recommend a wine unless you know its qualities.
- Do not cool a wine by placing ice in the glass.
- Never use soap or soda when cleaning a decanter, but use warm water

and small lead shot, or raw potatoes diced, and allow the decanter to dry before using it again.

- Keep stoppers off decanters after they have been washed in order to allow the inside to dry thoroughly.
- Use clean glasses when serving a second bottle of the same kind of wine.
- Always wash glasses in hot water, rinsing in clean, hot water and then polishing with a glass cloth.
- A glass should not only be clean, but beautifully clean.

Principal wines

French

Champagne	From the district around Rheims.
Bordeaux	Red: known in England as Claret.
	White: Graves, Sauterne, Barsac.
Burgundy	Red: Burgundy, Côte d'Or, Beaujolais, etc.
	White: Chablis, Pouilly, Meursault, etc.
Côtes du Rhône	Red: Burgundy type.

Alsatian   White: Moselle type.

German

Hock	White: Rhine wine.
Moselle	White: Moselle.

Spanish

Sherry   Derives its name from the town of Jerez
Also many table wines

Portuguese

Port	Fortified wine from the area of the River Douro.
Madeira	Fortified wine from the Island of Madeira.

Italian

Chianti	Tuscany.
Asti	Sparkling, Piedmont.
Lacrimae Christi, etc.	Naples and southern Italy.

Other countries

Australia and   Produce red and white wines similar
  South Africa, USA,   to claret, port, hock,
  South America   burgundy and sherry.

Hungary, Austria,
  Yugoslavia, Greece,
  Russia (Black Sea)   Various type of wine.

Service of other drinks

The aperitif

This appetizer before a meal aims to stimulate the palate. It is usually taken in the lounge or bar, however the restaurant customer often likes one at table.

Sherries, 'dry', 'medium' or 'sweet' are often asked for by name. Some visitors prefer Dubonnet, Campari, Vermouth, Pernod or other sweeter aperitif wines. Learn the ingredients of a few popular cocktails to assist you in taking an order.

On seating a party, first ask the host if he would like a sherry, cocktail or other aperitif. Serve these as quickly as possible so that they can be enjoyed while the meal order is taken.

As these drinks are served in the glass:

- Carry them on a cloth-covered wine salver in case of slight spillage during carriage.
- If the base of the glass is wet on arrival at the table, clear it by rubbing a finger off the base onto the cloth. Picking up a filled glass to wipe it can cause more spillage and possible accident.
- Change the cloth on the tray if it gets soiled.
- Place the glass on the table just below and to the right of the table glass, which should not be removed.
- When the drinks are finished, clear the glasses.

Cocktails

Mixing cocktails is a task for a trained barman. A waiter on lounge service or assisting at a pre-function reception should, nevertheless, know the ingredients of a few commonly demanded cocktails (see Table 13).

Table 13   Common cocktails and their ingredients.

Cocktail	Ingredients
Bacardi	White rum, lime juice, sugar, Grenadine
Bloody Mary	Vodka, tomato juice, lemon juice, Worcester sauce, salt, pepper
Brandy sour	Brandy, lemon juice, sugar, cherry garnish
Champagne cocktail	Champagne, brandy, bitters, lemon peel
Coladas	Cane spirit and/or rum-based drinks with, say, coconut and other flavourings

Daiquiri	As Bacardi (without Grenadine)
Gin and Dubonnet	Gin with Dubonnet aperitif wine
Gin and Italian	Gin with Italian vermouth
Gin and French	Gin with French vermouth
Manhattan	Rye whisky, Italian vermouth, bitters
Martini (dry)	Gin, French vermouth, olive garnish
Martini (sweet)	Gin, Italian vermouth, cocktail cherry garnish
Old-fashioned	Whisky, bitters, sugar, fruit garnish
On-the-rocks	Any liquor served neat poured over ice cubes
Rob Roy	Scotch whisky, Italian vermouth, bitters
Screwdriver	Vodka and orange juice on ice cubes
Sidecar	Brandy, Cointreau, lemon juice
Whisky sour	Whisky, lemon juice, sugar, cherry garnish
White Lady	Gin, Cointreau, lemon juice

Service of beers

Bottled beers are usually served from 3 dl (half pint (10 oz)) bottles and poured into a 3.5 dl (12 oz) glass. As they are served with a 'head' or 'collar' (froth), do not delay serving. English beers are served at cool, cellar temperature. Lager beers (including British) are served chilled. Draught beers served in half pints (3 dl) or pints (6 dl) must be served in glasses, mugs or tankards bearing the official crown marking and quantity, and must be full to this mark.

Liqueurs

Liqueur glasses vary in size and shape according to the establishment, but usually have a line cut into the glass to mark the measure. Take the bottles to the table, present and pour the measure into the glass in front of the customer.

Liqueurs contain spirits (often brandy) and may be sweetened and flavoured with fruit, distillations of herbs, flowers and spices. They are believed to aid digestion. Some liqueurs are secrets of the monasteries after which they are named, they continue to be invented.

Liqueurs and their predominant flavours

Abricotine	Apricot
Advocaat	Yolks of egg and brandy
Anisette	Aniseed
Apry	Apricot
Aurum	Orange
Benedictine	Herbs and brandy
Calvados	Applejack brandy

Chartreuse (Green or Yellow)	Herbs and spices
Cointreau	Orange (white)
Crème de Cacao	Chocolate (usually served topped with fresh cream)
Crème de Menthe	Peppermint (green, white)
Curaçao	Orange
Drambuie	Herbs and honey (Scotch whisky-based)
Glen Mist	Irish whiskey-based
Goldvasser (Danzig)	White spirit, herbs and gold leaf
Grand Marnier	Orange
Izarra	Mountain herbs and brandy (Basque)
Kirsch (Wasser)	Cherry kernels (butter almond)
Kummel	Caraway seed
Tia Maria	Coffee and rum
Trapestine	Herbs and brandy (Abbaye Grace de Dieu)
Van der Hum	Herbs, bark, tangerine-orange
Vieille Cure	Herbs and brandy (Abbaye Cenon)

Service of liqueur brandies

Many customers prefer a liqueur brandy after a meal. Brandy is a distillation from wine. Freshly distilled brandy is raw, fiery and colourless. It mellows in flavour and acquires colour from maturation in cask. (Spirit, unlike wine, does not mature in the bottle.) As brandy is a spirit, there is constant evaporation and therefore loss of stock. The longer brandy is in cask the mellower and dearer it becomes.

Brandy is made all over the world, however French brandy is considered to be the best. France's finest brandy comes from Cognac, a defined area and only brandy made in this area can be called Cognac.

As brandy is enjoyed by bouquet as well as by taste, it is usually served in a brandy goblet. The large bowl (balloon) allows the glass to be wrapped in the hands to warm it through and release the aroma. The narrower neck traps this bouquet in the bowl for full appreciation. When serving brandy, whether in a 'balloon' or liqueur glass, quote the name, for example, 'Your Bisquit Dubouché, sir/madam'.

Knowledgeable brandy drinkers prefer to use their hands to warm their own brandy glass for if the glass is too warm, aroma is released too quickly and the brandy harmed. However, some customers ask for the glass to be warmed before putting in the brandy. Never do this without customer's permission. If a customer does require his glass warmed, never put it over a methylated flame. Brandy is delicate, takes in ulterior flavours easily and can quickly gain the smell of the methylated from a contaminated glass. To warm a glass, use hot water, afterwards wiping and polishing the glass thoroughly before pouring in the brandy.

Fruit brandies

Distillations made with other fruits and labelled 'brandy' such as cherry brandy, apricot brandy, peach brandy, prunelle (plum brandy) are liqueurs, not pure brandies, and are served as liqueurs.

Spirits

Spirits are more popular in bars, but may be ordered at table instead of wine and taken with mineral water.

Whisky   Scotch (preferred in this country), Irish (whiskey, spelt with an e), Rye from America and Canada, and Bourbon from America.

Gin   'London Dry', of various brands, is the most popular. Other gins include 'Plymouth' (less dry and used in pink gin, i.e. gin tinged with Angostura bitters), 'Hollands', 'Sloe'.

Brandy   Served as a long drink with soda water, this is usually a younger brandy than that listed as a liqueur brandy.

Spirits are usually served by measure, the customer ordering a 'single' or a 'double', often by brand. If this is not available, inform the customer and offer an alternative.

The most usual mixers asked for with spirits are:

whisky – soda water or similar aerated water,
            ginger ale or plain water (which should
            be iced).
gin   – tonic water and slice of lemon, ginger
            ale, ginger beer or plain iced water.
brandy – similar to whisky.

Service of spirits

Check your order and obtain the spirits in glass and bottled mineral from the dispenser.

- Carry the order to the table; glasses and bottles on a wine salver.
- Place the glasses on the table
- Ask the customer 'Would you say when, please, sir/madam', steadily pour in the mineral until told to stop
- Place the mineral bottle on the table if there is anything left in it.

Ice should always be available.

Service of soft drinks

Squashes

To serve bottled orange or lemon squash, etc.:

- Place drinking straws in a stand or in a glass on the table at time of service.
- Place the measure of squash in the glass with ice and fill up with water or soda water giving a light stir to mix properly.

Fresh fruit squash (e.g. lemon)

To make fresh fruit squash at the table:

- place on a wine salver the freshly squeezed juice in glass (tumbler), a bowl of caster sugar, a bowl of ice and straw stand and then carry to the table with the soda water and/or water as desired
- at the table, add sugar to the juice (to customer's taste) and stir to dissolve
- add ice and then slowly pour in the water or soda water, stirring lightly
- make certain the sugar is dissolved and that the soda is added carefully to avoid uncontrollable effervescence

Mineral waters

There are two types of mineral water:

Natural Spring waters which are bottled waters from spas such as Vichy Etat, Vittel, Contrexeville, Evian, Perrier, Malvern and Appollinaris.
Manufactured Waters such as soda water, and including flavoured varieties like ginger ale, ginger beer, tonic water, lemonade, and bitter lemon.
For service pour a quantity into the table glass and place the rest on the table.

Licensing law

A waiter is not expected to know all the details of licensing law, but he should understand how it is applied to his work. As ignorance of the law does not excuse breaking it, a careless waiter could unwittingly jeopardize his employer's licence.

Tobacco and its storage

Customers invariably order a brand of cigarettes or tobacco to which they are accustomed, but with cigars a waiter may be asked for his recommendation.

Reliable merchants make sure that tobacco they sell to a restaurant has been stored properly up to the date of sale. Tobacco is sensitive, easily absorbs moisture, and may take on any strong smell near it.

Tobacco should not be exposed to extremes of heat or cold or to wet or particularly dry air; otherwise the aroma is soon lost (particularly of cigars). A temperature of 18°C (65°F) is the most suitable.

Tobacco sales

If a large quantity of tobacco is sold, the restaurant will almost certainly have one member of staff responsible for ordering, storage, sales, records and passing of invoices. The waiter's work is then restricted to taking the customer's order, obtaining the quantity required and seeing that it is paid for.

- In many establishments the waiter will give in a special order to whoever is in charge of tobacco and obtain it in a manner similar to obtaining food from the kitchen; then enter the item on the customer's bill.
- In others, the customer is either required to pay cash at the tobacco kiosk or over the counter, or if you, as waiter, take the order, ask for the money and pay for it yourself, without any record being made on your own check book.

Offering a 'light'

As a waiter, see that a properly cleaned ashtray is on the table at the right time and that a light (match, not lighter is available. If ask for a 'light':
for a cigarette, strike the match (holding it away from the customer) and hold the flame to the cigarette.
for a cigar, hand the customer the box of matches.
In addition, have ready a cigar cutter. Connoisseurs of cigars prefer a cut end (either a deep V cut or straight slice) rather than a pierced end. The good 'flue' provided by the cut ensures a cool, free drawing of the smoke, whereas a pierced end becomes 'tarry'.

Cigars

Cigar quality depends on the tobacco; the best tobacco comes from the Vuelta Abajo district, number one, in Cuba where tobacco is more aromatic than anywhere else in the world.

Most cigar smokers like cigars to be mild. 'Strength' is determined by the 'filler', the tobacco making up the main part and around which the 'wrapper' or outer leaf is rolled.

Blenders, therefore, aim to make cigars of one brand as uniform as possible. Mild blends are made of the fine, ripe leaf. Full-flavoured ones are of the heavier leaf which has maximum body and aroma.

Cigars are made in many parts of the world; for example Havana, Java, Jamaica, India, Burma, Manilla and Mexico. Some excellent cigars are made in the Netherlands and Britain, but from tobacco imported from Havana, Jamaica, Brazil, Java and America. Often wrappers are leaf from Sumatra or Borneo, although Havana wrappers may be used on some brands.

A dark wrapper does not necessarily indicate a strong cigar and both light and dark wrappers may be bitter and strong if the tobacco has not been properly ripened and cured. Proper maturing takes from 6 months to 3 years.

Colour grading and size

Cigars are graded by the colour of the wrapper:

Claro:	light
Colorado Claro:	a little darker than Claro
Colorado:	darker still

Leading cigars sold in Britain are made in different sizes and shapes, for example Churchills, Lonsdales, Corona, Petit Corona, Half-a-Corona, Panatellas, Margaritas.

Quality and storage

Bear in mind the following points.

- Cigar ash is some indication of quality. A first-grade cigar produces greyish ash which lasts for a considerable time before falling.
- Do not put a cigar to the ear and crackle it. Although this indicates whether it is dry (which is important), crackling may break the leaf and damage the cigar.
- Cigars are usually sold in boxes of 25, 50 and 100. Cabinets are also provided, containing any number from 250 to 1000 in assorted sizes.
- An attractive box or band does not necessarily mean a good cigar, nor does the wrapper necessarily indicate that the important filler is of equal quality.
- To give reasonable choice to guests, keep cigars in a service cabinet in which there is a choice of three to six sizes ranging from good, moderate-priced cigars up to more exclusive and higher-priced ones.
- A good cigar depends on 'reputation', the quality of the tobacco in the filler and wrapper, its correct maturing, grading, rolling, storing and packing.

19
Checking, Control and the Bill

A checking system in restaurants is essential at every stage, properly to coordinate food and drink in order to present a correct bill to customers without delay. All items (table d'hôte or à la carte dishes, wines, liqueurs, tobacco or coffee) are only obtained by a waiter on presentation of a check (or voucher) for articles required.

Although fundamentally the same in all establishments, checking varies in detail according to the type of business done. A check is written proof that a customer has been served with the items he ordered. If a dispute arises, any mistake can be adjusted and the waiter or department concerned identified and dealt with.

Not all orders to the kitchen or dispense can be issued by word of mouth for chaos would result: bills would be wrongly made out; disputes would arise, pilfering on a large scale would take place; and the business would go bankrupt through lack of control. Therefore everything should be checked.

Breakfast procedure

One exception is that hotels making inclusive 'bed and breakfast' charges do not expect waiters to put in checks for breakfast dishes served. It takes too long and wastes too many check pads. Control is obtained through the kitchen returns, for example with 100 visitors, allow for 100 breakfasts.

Mechanization

For checking, many operations use machines operated either by service staff or a cashier (Figure 49). Machines are simply labour-saving devices used within a framework of established control principles.

Commonly in a basic mechanization, orders for food and drink are inserted in the machine and priced before issues are made. In operations with standard prices, the machine's numbered keys for each menu item may be pre-set with the price. The bill copy is inserted in the machine for totalling

Figure 49 A cash register machine, the Sheraton Park Tower restaurant, London. Courtesy of NCR Limited.

when payment is due. An advantage of mechanization is the availability of immediate analysis, summarizing takings broken down into various sectors of food and drink (providing ready analysis of sales and relative popularity of dishes), credit or cash sales and business done by different members of service staff.

A computerized ordering system can provide keyboard terminals for use by waiters, chefs, bar staff and management. All these can enter information through server terminals. Results, processed into stock and sales control figures, can be summoned up on a management console. Table orders keyed in by waiters print out on corresponding kitchen terminals. Dishes when ready are signalled to the waiter at his restaurant terminal. He can obtain a detailed bill when needed by the touch of a button.

Types of manual checking systems

Hand-written checking, however, is still used in many operations. The following outlines typical procedures.

À la carte   Every dish on the menu is priced separately so that every check order must state requirement and dish price. These checks are as important as if cash was passed. If omitted on the final bill, they can account for loss of revenue and waiter's 'shortages' (short payment).

Table d'hôte   As a complete meal or set of courses at a fixed price is charged, no prices need be mentioned, for example, simply 'Room 84, 4 lunches'. If the meal deviates from the set menu, the check is expected to show the different dish served and the customer can be charged extra at the head waiter's discretion.

Making out checks

Always write checks clearly and legibly to avoid mistakes and loss of time. Checks should bear:

- either the room number, or table (house custom)
- the date
- the waiter's station letter or number

The single carbon with perforation is used for table d'hôte or à la carte service with direct contact with the kitchen, one copy to kitchen and one copy on station, or to restaurant cashier (house custom).

The double carbon is used where two copies are needed and is almost exclusively for full à la carte restaurants. The original is generally sent to the kitchen to obtain the goods, one carbon remains on station and one carbon copy goes to the restaurant cashier for preparation of the ultimate bill.

The triple carbon includes one sheet of transparent paper (called a flimsy) so that the waiter has an original and two copies, to be used as described above. The flimsy remains either on the guests' table or the side-table, to remind the commis waiter what is the next course to be served. This system is used only in busy high-class à la carte restaurants where four people at the same table may all order entirely different dishes.

'Return' checks

For strict control, once a check has been handed in, it cannot be regained. If a commodity has to be returned for some reason, another check has to be made out marked 'Return' and sent with the dish in order to cancel the transaction. These checks should bear the head waiter's signature to prove their legality to 'control'. The waiter thus makes certain that the item is taken off the bill.

'En place'

On the table d'hôte a customer sometimes wishes for a slight change in a dish so an 'en place' check has to be made, for example '4 soles frites 'en place' fish du jour'. Although no money is involved, the head waiter signs to show that he has permitted alteration from the standard menu at no extra charge.

'En suite'

'En suite' check is also used when serving a table d'hôte meal. In most establishments the meal order is taken only as far as the main course. When the guest has eaten this dish and plates have been removed, the menu is again presented and the order for the sweet is taken. This check, which is headed 'en suite', shows the customer's choice as well as room or table number, date and waiter's signature or number.

Extra charge

Sometimes an extra charge is to be made, so the check could read '4 @ £9.75. Poulet Maryland extra £0.95'. Waiters must see that the extra charge is on the bill.

No charge (N/C)

Sometimes a waiter requires ingredients from various sources to finish a dish (which has already been charged the full price). As checks are necessary for all items to cover issue of stock he makes a check, for example, '2 Curaçao for Crêpes Suzette N/C', which is signed by the head waiter.

Cancellations

Usually checks have serial numbers and every check must be accounted for. If a check is spoiled in any way, it has to be cancelled and sent to 'control'. The waiter writes 'cancelled' across the check and it is signed by the head waiter. On no account should it be destroyed or thrown away.

Duplicates

If a check is mislaid, to save the customer waiting, make out another with 'duplicate' written at the top in case the first check gets through to 'control' and you, as waiter, are debited with two orders while only one is charged on the bill. This check requires the head waiter's signature to prevent dishonest usage.

Writing wine checks

To prevent complications and mistakes, wines are usually given a 'bin number' in the cellar and that number is quoted on the wine list, so the wine waiter orders his wines by the numbers only (see Chapter 18).

- The first figure denotes number and size of bottle.
- The second figure is the bin number.
- The total price is just underneath (which must be in pence).

If wines are returned to the cellar for any reason, a return check is made out with the reason marked on the check ('unopened', 'corked', etc.), and signed by the person authorized to do so.

Checking for other drinks

Spirits by measure should be written as numbers of measures and total price, for example '4 double whiskys @ 95 p a measure' should read: '8 whiskys 760 p'. This indicates to the cashier how much to charge; saves time and error in making up bills; and prevents friction from hurried accountancy causing 'shortages'.

If more than one item is written on the check, the total price should be written in and ringed. Well written, tidy checking avoids shortages which irritate the waiting staff.

Check minerals, beers and other open drinks in the same way.

Room number checking

When guests staying in a hotel take drinks in the lounges or bars, they often prefer to have their orders placed on their 'house bill'. As waiter:

- mark the check with the room number and send a copy to the 'bill office'
- politely ask the guest to sign the check (offer a pencil on the plate or salver)

This safeguards guests from drinks being charged unfairly and safeguards the waiter if a guest queries the amount when he eventually pays. If a guest refuses to sign, ask your head waiter to initial the check as a witness against possible dispute.

Café system

In smaller establishments a waiter may be responsible for taking his orders, collecting his items and eventually making out his own bill.

Bill pads have carbon duplicates and may be similar to the one illustrated in Figure 50. Pads are already printed and cash entries are made only against those items the customer has consumed.

At the end of the service the bill is handed to the control and the money paid over. This system has many disadvantages vis-à-vis the restaurant and its control.

Token system

The 'token' or 'counter' system is now only rarely used. The waiter is supplied with so many counters (chips) on starting duty. For every order taken he puts in an appropriate chip for the item he requires (sandwiches, tea, coffee, beer, etc.). No cash changes hands between the waiter and service. He serves his customers, makes his bills, and on being relieved of his station he pays into 'control' his takings, reckoned on the number of chips he has handed in, less the number of chips still in his possession. This system originated in beer restaurants in Europe where waiters were on duty for long hours.

The bill

On handing over your station to a relief waiter, leave everything paid on your station so that your relief takes over with a clear start. This resembles the 'change over' of conductors on buses, who are responsible for all tickets bought until their reliefs take over.

Bills are printed with the necessary data, and you or the cashier fill in the general amounts.

The à la carte bill usually shows the various courses with a section for

	£	p
BREAKFASTS		
4 LUNCHEONS @ 9.75	39	00
DINNERS		
SUPPERS		
WINES 1 x 57	7	40
MINERALS		
SPIRITS	7	60
BEERS		
LIQUEURS		
4 COFFEE	4	00
SUNDRIES: Extra for Chicken Maryland	0	95
	£ 58	95
Service 15%	8	38
	£ 67	33
W/L Table No. Date		
A 15 9/3/87		

Figure 50 An example of a table d'hôte bill.

wines, beers, minerals, coffee, etc. Make up the bill by totalling the checks for each course and entering the totals in the cash column opposite. Enter wines as ordered, but with amounts now in £ and pence, for example 1 × 57 £7.40.

The table d'hôte bill in Figure 50 shows at the top the name of the meal with the other items, for example wines, beers, etc. underneath.

Presenting the bill

Check that the bill is correct before presentation. Shortages diminish profits and over-charging harms an establishment's reputation.

Bills can be paid in two ways, either by:

- the customer to the waiter to the cashier, or
- the customer on leaving, direct to the cash desk

Timing the bill presentation varies with the type of restaurant.

- In a quick-service restaurant, after ensuring that nothing else is required, as waiter you can usually place the bill on the table at the left-hand of the host.
- In a more leisurely restaurant, service may be required after the meal so the bill must remain open until asked for; however do not lose time in presenting the bill once it has been demanded. Never give the impression that you are trying to get rid of a customer, either because other guests need the table or because the restaurant is nearly empty and you want to get home.

Payment procedure

- Fold the bill from bottom to top with the right-hand corner (the corner opposite the total) turned back, so that the total is not revealed. (This is simply that the guest may more easily open the bill to glance at the total.)
- Place it on a cash tray or plate.
- In restaurants where the guest himself pays at the cash desk, no further action by the waiter (other than the departure procedure below) is required. Otherwise:
- In other restaurants, when the guest places money or a credit card on the plate, take this to the cashier for action.
- Return the receipted bill (folded as above) with the change; again to the host's left.
- Do not give any sign of anticipating a gratuity, especially by lingering at or near the table.
- Do not remove the plate (with or without any tip) until guests leave the table, unless motioned to do so by the host.

- Acknowledge any tip, whatever its size, pleasantly by expressing thanks.

Cheques

Unless a guest is extremely well-known, payment by cheque should be supported by a bank card. If this is not produced, courteously ask the guest to do so. Take both card and cheque to the cashier. Once the bill is receipted by the cashier, return it to the guest in the usual way.

Credit cards

Bills are increasingly settled by credit card (Access, American Express, Barclaycard, Diners Club, Visa and many others). Be sure you know which are acceptable in your establishment.

When an acceptable card is proffered, the cashier prepares the billing pro forma in duplicate. Bring this with the bill and a ballpoint pen for the customer to sign. Then separate the flimsy from the main copy, hand the customer his copy (usually the flimsy), together with his credit card.

Departure

Warmth, friendliness and courtesy at departure is as important as at the time of welcoming. When guests begin to rise from the table, come forward to assist:

- Withdraw chairs (especially for lady guests).
- Help with ladies' coats, etc. (and gentlemen where applicable, but theirs will normally be in the cloakroom).
- Ensure that guests have left nothing on or under the table or on chairs (check, for example, that nothing is concealed by discarded napkins).
- Bid the party farewell in a clear, courteous and friendly manner.
- If any gratuity has been left on the plate (or on the table), again, irrespective of amount, acknowledge it with a 'thank you, sir', audibly and courteously.
- Wherever possible, escort guests to the door or to a point where a head waiter may escort the party to the exit.
- At the door, the maître d'hôtel (or his representative) should bid the guest farewell adding some courteous, friendly comment such as 'it has been a pleasure to serve you; I hope we may soon welcome you here again, sir'.

20
Function Waiting

Banquet success depends on preliminary organization. Each waiter must organize himself and his section to fulfil his role in the function. He should be aware of arrangements which precede the banquet as well as those which apply during it.

The following departments require prior notification of the function:

kitchen

restaurant (banqueting or function manager)

cellar

plate room

housekeeper

hall porter

stillroom

Apart from the 'special business sheet' normally sent to all departments each week, further forms giving information may also be sent from the manager's office a few days in advance of the function. For each department, staff require the following information.

Kitchen

- Date and time of function.
- Number of services required and number of covers per service. (Information supplied by the function head waiter.)
- Any other information required from the service point of view.

Plate room

The plate room also requires the above details to supply silver for the kitchen and also plates, cutlery and glasses.

They also need details of menu, number of services, how many on each service; or better still the sizes and types of silver for each course; if finger bowls or special glasses must be made available; and any other information to suit the occasion.

Stillroom

This department requires only information to provide adequately for rolls, butter, Melba toast, coffee and milk, that is, date, time, place and total number. The stillroom and larder need notification if tea, sandwiches and cakes or breakfast are to be served later in the evening or early hours of the morning, as they attend to this requirement.

Restaurant (Banqueting manager or function head waiter) (Figure 51)

Date and time of function and:

> number of covers to be served
> where to assemble
> where to serve
> details of menu
> plan of the tables
> list of guests
> drinks, apéritifs: wines, liqueurs, spirits and whether pre-ordered (booked) or cash
> cigars, cigarettes
> any other information

Factors affecting the items mentioned in the above list are as follows.

Number of covers

The number expected may not be the number that will actually be present. It

Figure 51 An example of a function room, the Great Room, Grosvenor House, Park Lane, London.

is difficult, if not impossible, to add covers at the time of the function without disorganizing both kitchen and service, thus accurate estimating must be received.

Where to assemble

Apéritifs and appetizers (Zakouskis) are served in a reception room. Place a few chairs around the walls so that the elderly may sit. Provide small tables with ash trays, for guests to deposit empty glasses.

Where to serve

This information is supplied with the table plan.

Menu details

Menu details are required for the function in the room. Figures 52, 53 and 54

Figure 52   A selection of lunch menus for functions, The Strand Palace Hotel.

Figure 53 A selection of dinner menus for functions, The Strand Palace Hotel.

illustrate different function menus. In addition, where necessary, details of the following will be required: appetizers to be served during the reception; tea, sandwiches and cakes to be provided later on during the evening; soup (or, in certain cases, breakfast) to be served on departure.

Reception

A banquet is usually preceded by a sherry or cocktail reception for which waiters may be required.

Cocktails may include gin and French vermouth with a stoned olive on a cocktail stick (dry martini); or gin and Italian vermouth with a cocktail cherry on a stick (sweet martini). Glasses of sherry make up the choice of drinks offered. In certain cases other drinks can be obtained on demand.

BUFFET MENUS

BUFFET A

Russian Egg with Anchovies
Smoked Mackerel Fillets
Roast Sirloin of Beef
Roast Spring Chicken
Sugar Baked Gammon
Stilton and Spinach Quiche
Tossed Salad
Assorted Salads
Assorted Dressings

* * *

Apple and Blackcurrant Pie
Black Forest Gateau
Strawberry Mousse

* * *

Coffee

BUFFET B
Minimum 50 persons

Poached Scottish Salmon
Roast Sirloin of Beef
Roast Norfolk Turkey
Honey Baked Gammon
Sea Food Platter
Asparagus Quiche
Tossed Salad
Assorted Salads
Assorted Dressings

* * *

Black Forest Gateau
Apple and Blackcurrant Pie
Lemon Cheesecake
Profiteroles and Chocolate Sauce

* * *

Cheeseboard

* * *

Coffee

As an additional item to either Buffet A or B,
HOT DISH

Beef Stroganoff and Pilaf Rice
Curry Cashmir and Pilaf Rice
Coq au Vin and Pilaf Rice

STRAND PALACE HOTEL
Strand
London WC2R 0JJ
Telephone: 01-836 8080
Telex: 24208

STRAND PALACE HOTEL

Figure 54 A selection of buffet menus for functions, the Strand Palace Hotel.

Small savoury appetizers include cheese straws, game chips, salted peanuts and cocktail onions, arranged in small dishes around the reception room for guests to help themselves. Savoury canapés, however, are sometimes handed round by waiters. Half an hour is normally allowed for the reception.

Drinks

A special reception bar is usually set up to facilitate service in or near the reception room with a barman or a wine waiter in charge. Stock for this bar is drawn directly from the cellars.

The function head waiter must be informed about any special licence for this function as he is responsible for seeing that no drinks are served after the time limit.

Wines, apéritifs and other drinks can be paid for either by those giving the function or by each individual guest. Figure 55 is an example of a function wine list and bar tariff.

WHITE WINES

BURGUNDY
195	Macon Blanc Villages, Louis Latour 1983/84	£13.75
212	Rully, Bouchard Pere et Fils 1983	£14.00
214	Petit Chablis, J. Moreau 1984	£15.50
176	Montagny, Tête de Cuvée, Louis Latour 1983	£15.75
172	Meursault, Jaboulet-Vercherre 1983	£18.50
213	Chassagne Montrachet, M. Amance 1982	£21.50

BORDEAUX
72	Mouton Cadet Blanc, Baron Phillipe 83/84	£11.50
93	Graves, André Lucien N.V.	£11.50

LOIRE
285	Muscadet Sur Lie, Domaine Jousselinière, Sevre et Maine, 1983/84	£12.00
287	Vouvray, Choyer 1983/84	£12.00
292	Sancerre, Choix du Roy 1984	£12.75
294	Pouilly Fumé, de Ladoucette 1983/84	£16.00

ALSACE
274	Riesling, Camille Meyer 1983	£12.00
271	Pinot Blanc, Hugel 1983/84	£13.00
275	Gewurztraminer, Camille Meyer 1983	£14.50

ITALY & SPAIN
363	Soave Classico, Azienda Flli, Tedeschi 1983/84	£10.50
367	Frascati Superiore, Villa Catone 1983/84	£10.75
422	Torres Gran Vina Sol 1983/84	£12.50

RHINE
229	Niersteiner Gutes Domthal 1984	£10.50
223	Rudesheimer Rosengarten, Nahe 1983/84	£10.50
226	Liebfraumilch Blue Nun, Sichel & Sons 1983/84	£12.00
230	Liebfraumilch Crown of Crowns, Langenbach 1983/84	£12.75

MOSELLE
259	Piesporter Michelsberg Green Crest 1983/84	£11.50
267	Bereich Bernkastel Green Label, Deinhard	£11.75
255	Piesporter Goldtropfchen, Riesling, 1984	£13.50
260	Trabener Wurzgarten, Riesling Spatlese 1983	£13.75

GROSVENOR HOUSE RECOMMENDS
86	Sauvignon Blanc, Bordeaux 1984	£9.50
138	Beaujolais, 1983/84	£9.50
335	Crozes Hermitage Blanc, 1983	£13.50
679	Chateau du Clos Renon, Chateau Bottled 1978	£13.50

CHAMPAGNE
1	Ayala Château D'Ay N.V.	£18.00
20	Charles Heidsieck N.V.	£19.00
55	Tattinger Brut N.V.	£20.00
35	Lanson Black Label N.V.	£20.00
2	Ayala Château D'Ay 1979	£21.00
4	Bollinger N.V.	£23.00
39	Moet & Chandon 1980	£23.00
37	Moet & Chandon Rosé 1980	£30.00
59	Dom Perignon 1978	£50.00
58	Tattinger, Comtes de Champagne 1976/79	£55.00

SPARKLING
65	Bouquet D'Or, Brut, N.V.	£12.00
68	Blanquette de Limoux, Methode Champenoise	£13.50

HOUSE BRAND BOTTLE PRICES
Johnnie Walker Red Label	£29.00
Beefeater Gin	£29.00
Vladivar Vodka	£29.00
Bacardi Rum	£32.00
Calem Vintage Character Port	£16.50
Camus *** Cognac	£32.00

PROPRIETARY BRAND BOTTLE PRICES
Vermouth	£18.00
Sherry	£18.00
Campari	£26.00
Whisky, Gin, Vodka	£31.00
***Brandy, Rum	£34.00
V.S.O.P. Brandy	£43.00
Johnnie Walker Black Label, Chivas Regal	£43.00
XO Brandy	£47.00

CIGARS
Havana Coronas	Romeo & Julieta	£4.50
	Monte Cristo No 3	£4.75
Havana Petit Coronas	Partagás	£3.50
	Romeo & Julieta	£3.95
	H.Upmann	£3.50
Jamaican Petit Coronas	Macanudo	£3.00

RED WINES

BURGUNDY
102	Bourgogne Rouge Comtes De Chartogne, Jaboulet-Vercherre 1981/82	£12.50
131	Brouilly, Les Grumelles, Mommessin 1984	£12.50
143	Beaujolais Villages, Louis Latour 1983/84	£13.00
148	Fleurie, Château de Fleurie, Jean Loron 1983/84	£13.00
135	Côte de Beaune, Louis Jadot 1983	£16.00
136	Gevrey Chambertin, Louis Jadot 1982	£23.00

BORDEAUX
786	Bordeaux de la Maison, Paul Deloux N.V.	£10.00
785	La Tour Canon, Bordeaux Superieur, 1983	£11.00
781	St Emilion, Paul Deloux 1982/83	£12.00
783	Mouton Cadet, Selection Rothschild 1982/83	£12.50
658	Château La Rose Puy Blanques, St. Emilion 1981/82	£13.00
675	Château Lyonnat, Lussac, St Emilion 1981	£14.50
678	Château La Croix Bellevue, Lalande de Pomerol 1981/82	£15.00
633	Château Rauzan Gassies, 2 eme Cru Margaux 1979	£20.00
641	Château Ducru Beaucaillou, 2 eme Cru St. Julien 1976	£27.50

RHONE
341	Côtes du Rhone, Paul Deloux 1984	£10.50
349	Châteauneuf du Pape, Choyer 1983/84	£12.75

ITALY & SPAIN
384	Valpolicella Classico, Azienda Flli. Tedeschi 1981/82	£10.50
380	Chianti Classico, San Felice 1982	£11.00
433	Torres Gran Coronas, 1979	£13.50

ROSE
413	Mateus Rosé N.V.	£10.50
408	Tavel Rosé, Domaine de Roc Epine 1983/84	£12.00

PORT
319	Taylor's Late Bottled Vintage Reserve	£18.95
320	Calem 10 years old	£20.00
323	Smith Woodhouse 1970	£24.00
303	Fonseca 1970	£32.00

When stocks of any particular vintage become exhausted, the best available year is offered with every confidence.

Figure 55   The banqueting wine list and bar tariff, Grosvenor House, Park Lane, London.

Pre-payment

There are two alternatives: either the organizer orders beforehand and stipulates how many bottles; or each guest orders what he wants. Both the guest and the waiter serving the drinks, sign the checks.

Cash sales

For 'cash drinks', the guest orders what he wants and pays for it himself. A limited wine list is often used.

Drinks at table

As for apéritifs, organizers of functions may decide that for wine a limited number of glasses will be paid for by them (usually one for each guest); the rest to be on cash basis.

Liqueurs and spirits can also be obtained and paid for by the organizer or by individual customers.

Cigars and cigarettes

Cigars and cigarettes are sometimes provided by the organizers and handed to the head waiter at the time of the function. These can also be ordered by organizers when the function is first booked, in which case, the function head waiter must be notified. He then draws his requirements from the stores on the morning of the function.

Cigars are passed in boxes by wine waiters at a large function, or by the function head waiter at a small one. Cigarettes in glasses or boxes (a dozen or so in each) are placed at intervals on tables after the Loyal Toast (of the Queen).

Table plan

It is usual to have three or four alternative standard seating plans for each room used for this type of business. Ask organizers to select one of those plans instead of using one of their own. This is because in arranging seating an organizer may forget to take into account such factors as doors, windows, pillars, all of which affect the service.

'House' tables plans referred to as A,B,C, and D and so on must all have been tested; either by careful calculation and planning or by actually putting the tables in position. Sizes of banqueting tables and cloths must be taken into consideration when drawing up a plan.

Display one or two copies of the table plan for the guests in the reception room. For a large function, each table on the plan carries either a letter or a number. Next to this plan is a list of guests in alphabetical order, to indicate by letter or number where the guest is seated. Only in special circumstances are actual seats numbered at table, other than the top table. At the top table, each guest is informed of his place, usually by a name card at his (or her) seat. This information is previously advised by the organizers.

The table plan is usually displayed in the reception room to afford a guest maximum advance notice of where he is sitting.

Wedding seating

At a wedding function, seat:

bridegroom's mother and bride's father to her left
the bride's mother and bridegroom's father to her right
best man and the bridesmaid either next to or opposite the bride and bridegroom (dependent on the table arrangement) and the number of guests

WEDDING TABLE PLAN

Bridesmaid	Best man	Bridegroom's mother	Bride's father	Bride	Bridegroom	Bride's mother	Bridegroom's father

The officiating clergyman is normally seated near the head of the table.

Mise en place

A complete mise en place of all material required is essential. All cutlery must be on the table or on the waiter's service sideboard. (This latter applies to fruit knives and forks for dessert which are not set on the table until required.) Wine glasses that are to be used must also be on the top table; except liqueur and brandy glasses which remain on the wine service sideboard until required.

Place setting

Cutlery and covers are laid as for table d'hôte dinner (usually a full range) Glasses can be arranged either:

- in a straight line across the top of the joint knife in the order in which they are going to be used, starting from the right with the sherry glass and finishing with the port glass, or
- in the form of a triangle, the sherry glass being the pivot. Glasses to be used first are placed to the right, others to the left.

Guest and staff numbers

Sometimes a function organizer asks the head waiter to check on numbers present at the function and to notify him of that number as soon as possible during the meal.

The number of waiters or waitresses required both for drinks and food service have to be decided upon in advance. A usual quota is:

one food waiter for each ten guests
one wine waiter for each 25 guests

Space and guests per waiter

Seating by the table plan (according to the room's size, shape and number to be accommodated) allows a minimum space of 140 cm ($4\frac{1}{2}$ feet) between each table for the chairs and a space wide enough for a waiter to serve.

Banqueting table size may vary when made to specification, but usually accommodate three to six guests on either side.

The space required for each cover is 70 cm (28 inches) minimum to 80 cm (32 inches) maximum.

A waiter may, therefore, have to work in a limited area.

Announcing the meal

At the reception (or in the ante room), on receiving the signal from the organizer or chairman, the toastmaster or announcer bangs his gavel three times and says 'Mr Chairman, My Lords (or other titles in order of importance), Ladies and Gentlemen, dinner (or luncheon) is served' in a loud, clear and formal voice.

A toast list will have to be provided if an announcer or toastmaster is required for the reception or for the dinner.

Dining room preliminaries

When the doors of the banqueting hall are opened, guests take their seats at table. In some cases, top-table guests do not enter the banqueting hall until all other guests have found their places. Then the announcer adds when announcing the dinner 'with the exception of the top table, will guests kindly proceed to the banqueting hall'. On such occasions, all guests stand when top table guests enter and only resume their seat when everyone at the top table is seated.

During these preliminaries, waiting staff stand to attention at their respective stations.

The announcer now calls guests to attention by banging three times with the mallet saying 'Mr Chairman, My Lords, Ladies and Gentlemen, pray silence for the Reverend X_____ (or Mr X_____) who will say grace'.

Once this has been done the meal begins.

Banquet service

A banquet menu usually has four, five or, sometimes, more courses (Figure 56).

Each waiter is allocated a number of covers: from eight to twelve according to the function's importance, a wine waiter up to 30 or 35 covers.

Timing and movement

Waiters clear and serve together as a drilled team during the meal service.

Staff movements are directed by the function head waiter, who signals to the waiter serving the chairman to begin serving or clearing.

Other waiters when not actually serving must stand at the foot of their station constantly keeping an eye on the top table as well as their own station.

They must not lean against walls, pillars or furniture, nor enter into conversation with one another.

Wine waiting

Wine waiters have greater freedom of movement

- They go in and out of the room for customers' orders when drinks are on a cash sales basis.
- When wines are pre-booked, wine waiters receive one or two bottles of wine each of the first one to be served.
- They do not receive more of that wine, or of other wines to be served, unless they return the first bottles they have received, whether empty or not.

BANQUET

Huîtres impériales d'Ostende
Consommé des viveurs en tasse

Langouste froide à la parisienne

Mignon de boeuf favorite

Neige au Champagne

Poularde de Bruxelles dorée
à la broche
Salade Lorette

Surprise d'Hawai

Mignardises

Moka

Magnums G. H. Mumm Cordon Rouge 1937

Figure 56 An example of a traditional dinner banquet menu.

- Control on wines hinges on the fresh bottles being supplied only on the return of an equal number of empty or partly empty ones.

Toast procedures

The function head waiter or the toastmaster (or announcer) normally stand behind the chairman during the meal and during the speeches following. At the meal's conclusion, when coffee cups have been placed before the guests, the toastmaster calls attention with his gavel and announces:

'My Lords, Ladies and Gentleman, pray silence for your chairman who will propose the Loyal Toast'.

As soon as this has been done, wine waiters place ash trays on tables.

This toast is an indication that the formal part of the meal is over. Guests are now allowed to smoke.

When coffee has been served (immediately after the loyal toast), the food waiters have their coffee pots and milk jugs re-filled. After a reasonable length of time, coffee is passed again. After this, coffee cups are cleared and the food waiters leave the room for good. Wine waiters only now remain.

The speeches and replies which follow are announced by the toastmaster:

'Mr Chairman, My Lord (if any) Ladies and Gentlemen, pray silence for Mr X_____, who will propose the toast . . .'

(of the Association, for example) or 'who will give the reply . . .'.

Wine waiters taking over

At this stage, wine waiters have taken over from the food waiters. They complete all the service that is required.

Wine waiters move quietly among the tables serving drinks. (Glasses must never be empty during this period of toasting.) They change ashtrays frequently (covering the used ashtray with the inverted clean one, removing both together and replacing with the clean). Under no circumstances should a waiter go round with a plate on which merely to empty dirty ashtrays.

Index

pests, 50
petite marmite, 129
pineapple, serving, 142
place mats, 78
place settings *see* covers
placing, 90
plat du jour, 93
plate service, 103–4
plates, 69
  for covers, 81–2
  placing, 115
  polishing, 112
  putting on table, 115
  removing, 116–17
  types, 69
plover eggs, 126
polishing
  cutlery, 68–9
  plates, 112
  silver, 68–9
potatoes cooking styles, names, 33–4
poultry
  accompaniments, 133–4
  carving, 148–50
  items, names, 31
  in season, 11
preparation, pre-service, 57–9
private house service, 100
problems, possible, 92, 120–1
  preventing, 122

quick service, 120

reception desk, 61
receptions, 208–9
  tea, 178–9
relaying covers, 86
relevé, 20
remove, 20
reservations, table, 90
restaurants, 1–5
  ambience, 2–3
  brand names, 4
  checking, 72–4
  entrance, 72–4
  ethnic, 4
  fast food, 4
  furniture, 61
  gourmet, 4
  maintenance, 74
  personality, 4
  as sales area, 1–2
  supervision, 41
  types, 1, 3–4

rice *see* pasta
Ritz restaurant, 2
roast (rôt) course, 20
room number checking, 201
Russian service, 101–2

salads, 136–7
  dressing, 136–9
  service, 136
salmon, smoked, 125, 144
sandwiches, 175
sauces, 35–7
savoury course, 21
  savouries, 140
Savoy, menus, 18–19, 23, 175
seafood cocktails, serving, 125
seasonal foods, 11–12
seating guests, 91–2
sequence of service, 106–7
service
  aims, 97
  forms, 98
  order of, 106–7
  routine, 118
  rules, 98, 113–17
  sides, 113–14
  staffing for, 104–5
  styles, 97–104
  techniques, 107, 119–20
  tools, 107–13
service cloth, 111–12
service room *see* pantry
service spoon and fork, 108–9, 144
serving
  rules, 113–17
  from silver, 114–15
Sheraton Park Tower restaurant, 198
shrimps, potted, 126
sideboard work, 107
sideboards (dummy waiter), 62–3,
    75–7
  check, 76–7
  lay-up, 75–7
  stock, 76
side-table *see* guéridon
Silver service, 102, 108
  putting on plates, 115
  semi –, 102–3
silverware, 66–9
  care, 68
  cleaning, 68–9
  for drinks, 67
  for food, 67
  lay-up, 77